A THOUSAND ACORNS

A Thousand Acorns

By

Tom Hall

&

Chris Erickson

ISBN: 9798719040097

Table of Contents

Introduction · 1
Meet Tom and Chris · 3
Tom's Childhood ·11
Chris's Childhood ·21
Roosevelt High School · 39
Sandy · 43
California ·51
Back to Minnesota ·55
The Cardiologist · 63
A Summer School Course · · · · · · · · · · · · · · · · · ·67
Growing Inside, Outside · · · · · · · · · · · · · · · · · ·71
No More Coach Hall ·91
Irondale High School · 97
Sharing Life's Experiences · · · · · · · · · · · · · · · · ·103
The Day After Graduating · · · · · · · · · · · · · · · · ·119
A New Beginning: May 26th, 1979 · · · · · · · · · · · · ·129
Discipleship ·139
Our Ministry and Chris's Baptism · · · · · · · · · · · · ·149
Our Teaching Careers ·155
Chris's Calling ·169
Attacks from the Enemy · · · · · · · · · · · · · · · · · ·181

Marriage and Ministry · · · · · · · · · · · · · · · · · · · 189
Christina, Jessica and Michaela · · · · · · · · · · · · · · 197
The Farm and Divorce · 211
Lisa · 217
Tom's Retirement · 227
Where We're At Today · · · · · · · · · · · · · · · · · · · 233
Reflections · 247
Conclusion · 251
Afterword: An Unexpected Ending · · · · · · · · · · · · · 255
Appendix: Chris's Last Letter to Tom · · · · · · · · · · · 271
About the Authors · 275

AUTHOR UNKNOWN

I wish that I had been the kind of friend
That you have been to me.
To be the help you have been,
That you've always been glad to be.

To mean as much to you
Each minute of each day
As you have meant, old friend of mine,
To me along the way.

To have done the big things,
The splendid things for you.
To bring the gray from out of your skies
And leave them only blue.

To say the kinds of things
That I so often heard,
And feel that I could rouse your soul
The way that mine you stirred.

I am thinking at this saddened time
That I could but reply,
A portion of the gladness
That you have strewn my way.

Could I have one wish right now
This only would it be,
I wish that I had been the kind of friend
That you have been to me.

Introduction

Everyone needs a friend. A friend can be described as an intimate associate. Proverbs 17:17 states, "A friend loves at all times, and a brother is born for a time of adversity." Talk about a dichotomy. Are not brothers born to love each other? Proverbs 18:24 asserts, "One who has unreliable friends soon comes to ruin, but there is a friend who sticks closer than a brother." How would you define "friend?" How would you define "best friend?"

It takes time and energy to establish a friendship with another individual. Common interests bring people together and serve to cultivate a friendship. As these common interests bring us together and we communicate with each other, we share our experiences. As this takes place, we get to know the other person more intimately. Over time, our sharing becomes more genuine, honest, and transparent.

Through a summer school course involving a week-long wilderness canoe trip and camping experience, a teacher named Tom Hall and a student named Chris Erickson met and developed a lifelong friendship. When they first met, Chris was a wild 16-year-old and Tom was an experienced 31-year-old teacher. Tom is now 78 years old and Chris is 62. The two have known each other for 47 years! This is their story.

Meet Tom and Chris

Hi, I'm Tom.

Hey, I'm Chris. Tom and I have often joked about writing a book about our amazing friendship. He's the author after all! Tom has authored five books. His second book, entitled Growing Inside Outside, is a compilation of the ten wilderness canoe camping trips he took with students during the summers from 1971 through 1975. He used me as the main character in this book and included some of the actual experiences we had on two of those trips.

After the first canoe trip Chris and I took as teacher and student, circumstances seemed to draw us to each other and we began to spend time together. We both loved nature and enjoyed the splendor, freedom, and solitude of Northern Minnesota in the Boundary Waters Canoe Area (BWCA).

I'm Minnesotan born and raised and I had never heard of the BWCA before going on my first canoe trip with Tom. It's a

unique wilderness area right in our back yard that I grew to love, enjoy, and treasure in my heart.

My relationship with Chris began as soon as I met him when he was an energetic young 16-year-old.

In the introduction above it reads "wild 16-year-old." That was a long time ago. Forty-seven years to be exact!

When we first met at the initial meeting for the summer school course, I knew I wanted Chris in my group. I pushed to make that happen when my colleagues and I divided up the students to form three groups that would learn camping and canoeing skills together.

That's right. The first time I walked into that classroom at High View Junior High in New Brighton, Minnesota, we made eye contact and I just knew this Tom guy was the one I wanted as my leader. It was like magic at the time. Nothing was said, but a strong connection was made and I was suddenly invested in the course.

Over the next seven years, my relationship with Chris grew through moments when we would go out for coffee and talk about life. I think I was the one who weaned him onto coffee.

Yep, you sure did! I'm still enjoying coffee today, but with a lot less cream and sugar!

I was able to connect with Chris at first through the outdoors, but we later discovered a mutual love for the game of hockey. Chris was an excellent hockey player. He made Irondale High School's varsity hockey team as a sophomore and skated for my older brother Dave, who was the varsity hockey coach at the time. Chris and I didn't connect the dots about my brother Dave until after we were on the bus headed up north to Grand Marais, Minnesota.

I knew Mr. Hall before I met Mr. Hall!

Funny, Chris! When I was younger, our doctor's name was Dr. Wall. He had just finished giving me a physical examination one day when he stated, "I'd rather be you than me." I asked him what he meant. He replied, "It takes two walls to make a hall!"

Cute, Tom. Tom's brother Dave was a stand-up guy. He taught an electronics course at Irondale, which I took when I was a sophomore. I really didn't understand all that stuff about diodes and circuitry, so I goofed off a lot in class to cover my ignorance. Dave, "Mr. Hall" at the time, took me out into the hall one day, literally threw me up against the wall and read me the riot act something fierce. I actually respected him for doing that.

I liked how you worked two halls and a wall into that paragraph, Chris.

Totally unintentional.

Chris and I learned to trust each other. The quality time we spent together helped us get to know one another. Listening to each other helped us grow closer together. When problems came up, we encouraged and supported each other, which deepened the bond that was growing between us. As we grew in our relationship, we focused on understanding and answering each other's questions. Our care and concern for each other developed as we got to know each other better. We placed no demands on each other. When we saw each other after some time went by, we just picked up where we left off. We freed each other up by allowing the friendship to grow and develop naturally. We had each other's back and always supported each other.

Tom has always been better at the above than I have been. He would invite me into his home for dinner, take me out for coffee, and spend time with me when I would drop in on him at Pike Lake Elementary School where he taught fifth grade. I was pretty wild throughout high school and college and was doing a lot of things I shouldn't have been doing, but he either didn't know about those things or simply looked past them. Tom saw something in me I didn't see in myself. I knew Tom was different, but I didn't know what made him that way.

The differences in our ages was not a factor. I just happened to have a little more life experience than Chris did. We each had highs and lows in our lives. We would discuss them, seek advice, and share answers with one another. Eventually, we both shared the same careers as public school teachers. We discussed how to relate to students and grow in our careers as teachers. It was a wonderful friendship that eventually reached a plateau. Then something drastic happened in each of our lives. I experienced the passing away of my older brother Dave and Chris went through the loss of his best friend Jay.

God used both of our experiences with the death of people close to us to draw us to Himself. Without God in the equation, death doesn't make any sense.

Before these tragic experiences, I graduated from high school and invited Tom to my graduation party. He came bearing a wrapped gift. Inside the gift was a Zebco fishing reel. My dad taught me how to fish using what was called a drop line. When I went on that first canoe trip, I was amazed when Tom thought it was funny that I was using a drop line to fish. Laughing, he put a rod and reel into my hands, taught me how to cast, and then took me fishing in a bay on Lake Saganaga where I caught the biggest fish I had ever seen. It was a ten-pound Walleye as long as the blade of a wooden canoe paddle! Tom sparked my love of fishing and later golfing when he gave me his old set of golf clubs. I'm still using them today.

I kept in touch with Tom after going off to Rockford College in Rockford, Illinois. I would write to him and he would write back. As I was doing my thing at college, he was doing his thing at home. We would get together when I was at home on breaks or for the summer. We even painted houses together for a summer job. Working together like this revealed our weaknesses, especially mine. Like a cocky young know-it-all, I strode over to Tom while we were painting a house and informed him that he needed to redo a window that he painted. Tom, with

a tinge of a smile, very casually told me that I had painted that window. We have laughed over that incident many times over the years. He often flipped the bill at a Dairy Queen or another restaurant while I was home for a break during college. Tom would take me to a gas station, have me fill my tank with gas just before I had to go back to college, and then pay for it! He had a friend who owned a sporting goods store in Stillwater, Minnesota. We would go there and get all sorts of deals on clothing and sports equipment. Then he would take me out to eat at Brine's, a local butcher that served up some very tasty roast beef sandwiches. I remember saying to Tom that I could never repay him for all that he was doing for me. He simply replied, "Someday you'll return the favor either to me or someone else." I didn't understand what drove that kind of generosity.

At the time, Chris didn't understand that I was a man of faith. I had never shared my faith with Chris through words. I just never felt the opportunity was right to do that. He became my good friend and was, to a large degree, part of my family. Then one incredible evening, a month after I attended Chris's college graduation, Chris knocked on my front door. He never came to the front door. He seemed burdened as I invited him in, so we sat down and began a conversation. Chris unloaded on me all the bad things he was doing in life, stating that he wanted me to know the things I didn't know about him. Our conversation went late into the evening. I finally felt compelled to share my story with Chris. I talked about freedom and forgiveness. Chris listened intently. After a lengthy and deep discussion, Chris made the most important decision of his life in my backyard.

My life experienced a restart! This is our story which has persevered over a lifetime.

When life gets tough and you are laid low, a friend will come alongside and help. To have a friend that will support, comfort, encourage, empathize and stand with you in every circumstance is incredible. All of us need a friend like this when life gets tough.

We hope you enjoy our story. Really, the story of our friendship is just a part of God's story and how He can take lives like ours and infuse into them hope, security, and confidence. God uses people, things and events in our lives to draw each of us to Himself and helps us find our true identities in Him.

Tom's Childhood

One morning, Tom and I were standing at the counter in a McDonald's restaurant, and Tom was about to order a senior coffee. He asked me if I was old enough to have one. I remember just busting out laughing at the way he asked me with his signature little boyish grin on his face. It was the first time I realized I was old enough for senior discounts! So, Tom is going to share first about his background because he was born first and remains the senior of the two of us.

Thanks, Chris. Always remember, respect your elders.

My parents had two children and thought their family was complete. It was a perfect situation with a boy and a girl. Five years later, everything changed. My older brother Dave was seven and my sister Gwen was five when I came along. On a hot summer day on the eighth of August, Thomas Frank Hall was born.

This is the first thing Tom and I have in common. We are both third in our family birth orders.

My parents moved to a larger house in South Minneapolis. A few years after the move, Bob, Jon, Don and Steve were brought into the home. I heard my dad say at a later date, "All I did was hang up my pants on the bedpost and along came another child." Now we were a family of nine, which made life for the Halls quite interesting.

The second thing Tom and I have in common is that we both grew up in a family of nine. He had five brothers and a sister, whereas I had four sisters and two brothers. A third thing we have in common is that we both grew up in the city of Minneapolis. Tom spent his childhood in South Minneapolis, and I spent mine in Southeast Minneapolis.

Like Chris said, I'm the third child of Mr. and Mrs. Glenn Hall's family. This was a unique place for me. I was a little boy on the move. There were six boys and one girl in our large family. My brother Dave and sister Gwen were seven and five years older than me. After I came along, my younger siblings all arrived about two years apart. As a young kid I was a bundle of energy. My mom let me play in our backyard which was surrounded by a fence. However, if the gate was left open, I was gone!

I consider myself fortunate to have grown up under the supervision of Christian parents. My parents both loved God and loved each other. The relationship they had with each other gave us kids a great sense of security. When my dad would come home from work each day, he always greeted my mother with a hug and a kiss.

My dad was Lutheran and my mom was Catholic. They definitely loved each other. When my dad married my mom, he had to sign a paper agreeing that he would not interfere with his children being brought up Catholic. Go figure...I was brought up in the Catholic religion, but attended public schools.

My parents took us to church every Sunday. When we were young, they took us to First Baptist Church in downtown Minneapolis. As we grew older, my mom wanted us to go to church in the neighborhood. She decided that we would attend Grace Baptist which was just two blocks from our house. We could walk to church. We went to church every Sunday morning and evening, as well as the Wednesday night prayer meeting.

Wow...that's a lot of church! On Sunday mornings, my mom brought my brothers and sisters and me to St. Lawrence Catholic Church near Dinky Town by the University of Minnesota campus. It was like rounding up greased pigs trying to get us all out the door. We would fight all the way to church, attend the service, and fight all the way home. Well, maybe that didn't happen every Sunday, but it's what I remember the most.

When I was eight years old, my mom shared the gospel with her young sons, including me. She explained that God sent His Son Jesus to rescue us. I already knew I was a sinner and in need of a Savior. I prayed and asked Jesus to come into my heart that very day! I believe God answered my prayer. When I was 12 years old, I was baptized at Grace Baptist Church.

I never really heard the gospel message until I was 22 when you shared it with me. I was baptized as an infant. I can't remember it, but I have the paper to prove it happened. My Uncle Linus and Aunt Donnie were my godparents.

For the first nine years of my life, I lived in a closely-knit neighborhood. My best friend Bruce lived across the alley from me. We were together all the time. We were like two peas in a pod. We did everything together which usually involved action and movement of some kind. One day, when we were very young, we ran away from home together. The whole neighborhood was out looking for us. We showed up late in the afternoon and were both disciplined by our parents.

I ran away from home when I was four years old. I packed my little suitcase and walked out the front door of my home. We lived on the southeast corner at 13th and Talmage Avenue S.E. Halfway down the block, my suitcase accidentally flipped open and all my underwear came tumbling out right in front of this house where a girl I really liked lived...and she was sitting on the front steps! I was so embarrassed that I ran all the way home.

Funny, Chris! When I was ten, we moved to a new neighborhood about a mile away from our old house. I was not in favor of the move because Bruce and I wouldn't be able to see each other very often. However, we still remained good friends. Our new house was larger with more bedrooms. I occupied a bedroom with three of my younger brothers.

The good news about this move was that the house was located one block away from Sibley Park. I actually wrote a book about it and titled it Sib. Sibley Park was a place that became my home away from home. It was a safe place and provided lots of action for my boundless energy.

Van Cleve Park was my stomping grounds. Talk about home away from home! Sometimes my friend Jay and I each told our parents that we were sleeping over at the other person's house, and then we would stay out all night. We would sleep in the playground equipment at the park and then wake up to deliver papers for my paper route very early the next morning.

I got involved in sports and realized I had some athletic ability. In Minnesota, we have four distinct seasons. Each season has a specific sport. In the spring and summer, we played baseball. In the fall, we played football and in the winter, hockey. I developed friends by playing many team sports. In baseball, I was an outfielder. I had a strong arm which is important for an outfielder. I was also a pretty good hitter. In the fall, I played football. I was a quarterback on offense and a linebacker on defense. I enjoyed playing quarterback because I called all the plays. I also loved the hard contact playing defense.

Sports is another big thing Tom and I have in common. For me, it began at the park playing for the South East All Sports (S.E.A.S.). Like Tom, I also played baseball, football, and hockey. In baseball I played catcher, shortstop, and second base, but never pitched. I had a strong arm and stole a lot of bases. In

football, I loved to run the ball, played some quarterback, and was a safety. I loved the contact involved in tackling opposing players. For a little guy, I hit hard. I liked being able to see the whole field of play. In hockey, I scored a lot of goals and loved to fake out other players, pass the puck, and skate very fast forward and backward. Speed was my greatest asset in all these sports. I have a lot of trophies that the S.E.A.S program provided our teams with, some for special recognition and individual accomplishments.

OK, Chris, I'm trying to give my background, not yours.

Oh, yeah…sorry. I got a little carried away, didn't I?

Yep, but that's okay. I enjoy listening to you talk about the things you're passionate about.

Bruce lived much farther away from the park than I did, but he was still involved. He was a talented athlete and did very well in every sport we played. We fueled our friendship by playing sports together.

My first love was hockey! Bruce and I were at the skating rink every day during winter vacation. It didn't matter how cold it was. We were skating and playing hockey all day long. When my brothers and I were teenagers, my older brother coached us, and we became the city champions.

Growing up, most of my friends didn't know much about God, so I struggled fitting in because my conscience kept me from doing things I knew I shouldn't do. Although I was very silent about my faith journey, my friends knew there was something different about me. My parents and my church established a foundation for my life and God began a good work in me at a young age.

I've always remembered these words from Philippians 1:6 which says, "Being confident of this, that he who began a good work in you will carry it on to completion until the day of Christ Jesus."

This verse has had a great impact on my life, especially as I have grown older. Nevertheless, I grew up feeling lonely. I was not happy at church and felt separated from my friends because of my beliefs. Sports became my god and playing them gave me recognition. I especially excelled in hockey and absolutely loved it! God would later have to deal with that idol in my life.

Sports became my go-to pastime as well, but for different reasons. All those other things your friends were probably into, I was undoubtedly into as well...unfortunately. Without a compass, it's easy to get lost in the wilderness.

Something happened in my early teens that changed my life forever. When I was 13, my father died of a heart attack. It was an afternoon in the spring. I had just been at a friend's house and came home to see cars all around my house. I was confused about why we would have company because I knew my dad wasn't feeling well that day. Just then, my sister Gwen came outside and told me that my dad died. He was standing in the living room with one of my brothers who watched him fall down with a massive heart attack. The last thing he said was my brother's name, "Don..." I was shocked. I walked up to my room and cried myself to sleep. When I woke up in the morning, I was convinced that it was all a dream. It wasn't.

I loved and respected my dad. He was a great father and a wonderful husband. Honestly, I didn't know him that well. He was very busy working and providing for seven kids. However, I always knew he loved me.

I don't remember much about the funeral, but I do remember seeing my dad's open casket. I remember touching his body and knowing that he wasn't there; I knew that he was in heaven.

Growing up with no father caused a lot of bitterness and guilt in my life, as well as anger toward God and jealousy of my friends' situations. I felt guilty because I had not been an obedient son and I could never apologize to my dad or make it right. That burdened me for a long time. My life changed drastically as a young teen as a result of my father's death. I was forced to be the leader and role model for four younger brothers. Looking back, I really needed help in my teenage years. I needed counseling or something! I didn't really get over those emotions until my twenties.

After my dad died, my mom raised me and my four younger brothers all by herself. The five of us were the only kids still living at home at the time, and we were quite a handful! Fortunately, my dad had insurance that paid off our house. Many people gave my mom money at this difficult time to help us out. Although money was always an issue, somehow God always provided and the bills were always paid.

After my father's death, my mom went into depression for six months. This was really difficult for me as the oldest at home. She wasn't herself. She had been dependent on him for everything. This went on until one day, she suddenly snapped out of her grief. I think she realized she had five sons to live for.

God took care of our family. Our mom loved us and modeled her Christian faith to each of us every day. Although we all loved and respected our mom, she really had her hands full. We were not easy to raise! She would read a devotional to us called "Our Daily Bread." It was an outstanding devotional and I still use it today. Mom had a profound impact on all our lives.

My two older siblings, Dave and Gwen, have passed away but the rest of us are alive and well. I am now the oldest of my brothers. We own a summer cabin together and remain close.

All in all, I had a happy childhood. I was free and active with boundless energy and great outlets for it. I had a few close friends, a solid church, loving parents, and six boisterous siblings. Throughout my childhood, God always provided for my family.

Chris's Childhood

I was born on the morning of February 7, 1957, at St. Mary's Hospital in Minneapolis, Minnesota. Dr. Musty delivered me and weighed me in at seven pounds, eight and a half ounces. I was just over 21 inches long. My parents named me Christopher Allan Erickson. I was the third child of Edward and Grace Erickson. My parents brought me home to our house on top of a little hill in Columbia Heights, Minnesota, where my older sister Nancy Marie and my brother Jeffrey Thain awaited my arrival.

My grandpa, Lieutenant Colonel Joseph Lawrence Erickson, sent flowers to my mom with a note that read, "Heartiest Congratulations, Pap." He also mailed a postcard that was postmarked at 10:00 pm on February 7, 1957 from Austin, Texas. It read, "My dear little Christopher, I just received a telegram announcing your new arrival, which makes me very happy. This may be the first piece of mail you have received in this world. May the best of everything be yours in the future. Hope you and your mommy will continue to enjoy the best of health. Lovingly, Grandpa Erickson."

I recently discovered this postcard at the age of 62. No one chooses what family they are born into, but family, good or bad,

is the first influence that begins to shape your character and initially serves to determine who you are becoming. By reading my grandfather's note to me so many years after it was written, I learned that my Grandpa Erickson cared about me. He was one of the first to welcome me into this world, 62 years ago! His note was right there all along in a card sent to my mom, mailed on the day I was born. I can't even begin to explain how that affirmation echoing from generations past has made me feel.

I never knew my grandfathers. My grandmother on my mom's side died before I was born. She died of the flu at a young age. Her husband, my grandfather, went into a depression and became an alcoholic. My mother and her siblings were separated because my grandfather couldn't take care of them. My mother was the oldest at age nine and went to live with relatives in Goodhue, Minnesota. Her sister, my Aunt Gerry, lived with relatives in Walker, Minnesota next to Leech Lake. Her younger brother Frank, who I'm named after, was adopted by a couple in Wisconsin. When the three siblings grew up, they were able to forge a close relationship with each other as adults. As a result, I knew my mom's siblings very well as I was growing up in South Minneapolis.

That's amazing that the three siblings got together as adults after being separated from each other as children, a sad story with a good ending.

I learned some other things from the mail my mom received from others after my birth. I learned that my mom barely made

it to the hospital before giving birth to me. I guess I've always liked FAST!

My mom's family were all farmers of German descent. My mom had five sisters named Audrey, Justine, La Donna (Donnie), Jeanne, and Sheri. She also had a brother named Linus, who slipped into the family lineup of girls between Jeanne and Sheri. Sheri was my favorite aunt and the youngest of my mom's sisters. My mom, Grace Bernadine Hacker, was second in line of seven. They all grew up on a farm in southern Minnesota outside of Lafayette before moving to the big city of Minneapolis for school and work. Linus remained on the farm and worked the land. La Donna, Jeannie, and Sheri, all single at the time, were great aunts to me. They were always buying us Erickson kids Christmas gifts and frequenting our home to play cards and enjoy some socializing time with their sister. I'm not sure how they kept up with all the gifts, especially when my siblings Jane Louise, Ellen Beth, David Edward, and Britta Anne arrived on the scene.

My mom, after being separated from her dad, grew up on a farm and was the oldest of all the other kids in the family of her relatives. She did a lot of babysitting and they worked her very hard. I believe this is where she developed her strong work ethic. Through this experience my mom developed a very close relationship with all of the siblings she cared for on her relatives' farm. When they grew up and had farms of their own, we "city kids" would go visit them every summer. We loved it!

It's astonishing to me how many new things I'm learning about you as we write this book, Tom.

Linus, my mom's brother, introduced me to country life. I loved riding the tractors, playing in the hay loft and milking cows. I would spend one or two weeks on the farm with Linus and Grandma during the summer when I was growing up.

Wow, Chris, I guess we both loved visiting our relatives' farms as kids!

Like I said, we're learning new things about each other with every page we write!

My Grandma Hacker and Linus lived in a large two-story farmhouse that my mom grew up in. It was surrounded by a very nice hedge and landscaped yard. Inside was a large kitchen where my grandma prepared the tastiest food in large quantities. My favorite was big, huge slices of freshly baked bread hot out of the oven with butter smeared all over it. At the farm, there were always four meals. Breakfast was served very early, then lunch, followed by supper and finally a late dinner. Upstairs were the bedrooms and a bathroom with an old tub. My grandma would put about an inch of hot water in that tub and then expected us kids to bathe in it. An inch! In the basement of the house, my Uncle Linus had his train collection set on a table. The table filled the room with miniature railroad tracks laid out in an extensive network of routes that his trains would run on. It was an amazing collection.

There was always a collie on the farm that had free reign of the property. I especially loved one collie named Rex. He was a lot of fun, but he had a bad habit of chasing moving cars. Rex died chasing a passing car on the dirt road next to the hedge. He bit into a tire and broke his neck…at least that was what I was told.

I never had a dog growing up, or any animal for that matter.

I loved all the farm animals and my family had turtles, cats, rabbits, ducks, and dogs growing up. I'm sure this is where I get my attraction to animals, which really fed into the twenty years I spent on the hobby farm in Corcoran with my daughters where we had all sorts of animals.

The realities of farm life for this city kid began sinking in at a young age. Linus always denied this story, but when I was around eight years old, he had me kneel down one morning in the wet grass in front of the cow pasture and grab the wire in front of me. I did as he instructed and received a jolt through my being that I'll never forget. As Linus laughed, he said, "You'll never do that again."

And I never did. In a very practical way, Linus taught me what electric fencing was all about. He also introduced me to shotguns. When I asked him about his shotgun, he brought it out and loaded it. Then, Linus instructed me to bring it to my shoulder, point it out towards the field, and pull the trigger. I hefted it to my shoulder, pointed it towards the field, pulled the trigger… and nothing happened. Linus was laughing hard when he taught me about a mechanism called a safety. He

showed me how to engage the safety and disengage it. Making sure it was disengaged, I hefted the shotgun to my shoulder again and pulled the trigger. The next thing I knew, I was sitting on my behind! The blast had knocked me to the ground. I don't think I ever saw my Uncle Linus laugh so hard! I loved the sound of his laugh.

I have a scar on the top of my head from a car accident that occurred when I was five years old while riding to the farm with two of my aunts in Aunt Donnie's car. I was taken to the hospital in an ambulance. At the hospital, they shaved the top of my head and used a few stitches to close a cut I received when I went flying forward in the car and slammed my head into an ash tray on the dashboard. Those were the first of many stitches I received while growing up. In those days we didn't have seat belts and small kids could ride anywhere. I loved riding up front or curled up on the ledge in the back window of the car. That was the best place to sleep.

I loved doing that too! It was really fun to sit or lay wherever you wanted.

Memories from my dad's side of the family are more distant to me than those related to the farm and my mom's family. Some of my dad's relatives lived in the Minneapolis area. I remember Aunt Emmy, Uncle Gunard, and Clareen visiting our family or us visiting them. My dad and I would often go see old Uncle Elmer. I remember the cookies he would serve us when we visited and that his garage was immaculate. He also had giant ears! Most of the Ericksons all lived in Texas or some other part of the world.

I remember my dad's side of the family.

Go ahead, Tom.

My dad came from a family of six: four boys and two girls. We would have Christmas every year at his sister's house. We called her Aunt Myrtle. She lived with my grandma, who we all loved. I remember her Christmas tree because it had bubble lights on it. My dad and his brothers were all short with pot bellies and bald heads. They would tease each other and joke around. All the children loved witnessing their banter as it went back and forth, back and forth. When we grew up, all of the uncles came to our hockey games and sat in the same spot and cheered for us. They were proud of their nephews as we got many write-ups in the sports page. Walter, Roy, and Clarence were their names. They were hilarious, teasing each other mercilessly and then just laughing about it.

Sounds a lot like you and your brothers.

My dad was the youngest of four. He had an older brother named Earl and two older sisters named Carol and Leif. Leif married Squint and my cousins Corky, Jackie, Sherrie, and Buzzy followed. Squint was in the Navy and stationed at one time in Japan. Buzzy was born in Japan. I remember teasing him about that, which he did not like at all. If he would have known that a man named Dr. Musty delivered me when I was born, I'm sure he would have teased me as well. Earl married Kay and my cousins Mike, Suzy, Peter, and Eric followed.

I'm proud to be a Minnesotan. There's just something about growing up in Minnesota that tends to bring balance into your life. With four distinct seasons come four different sets of clothing needs, different foods, different jobs, and (my favorite) different sports. I remember starting to skate at the age of two on a pair of double runners that had buckles on the side. With the skates barely on my feet, I would slide from the top of the hill at the foot of my house in Columbia Heights to the neighborhood skating rink at the bottom of the hill. I don't ever remember my parents or my older brother or sister making that trip with me.

I vividly recall the very round, constantly smiling park attendant tightening up my skates for me and then matching me up with some older kids who would take me for the ride of my life on a saucer sled out on the rink, skates now firmly tightened and belted to my feet. After falling off the saucer at a high speed, I would go sailing across the ice and crash into a snowbank. I loved it! From there, I would scramble onto my double runners and find my way back onto the saucer for another joy ride. The fun would only stop when the older kids got tired or lost interest. Somewhere between two and four years old, I graduated to a regular pair of hockey skates. They were always previously used, but a little better than the ones I had before.

I refer to my family once in a while as a contesting family. My dad was a technical illustrator at Napco Industries in Hopkins, Minnesota, but on the side he entered contests. He played with developing jingles for companies to promote their products, but he also loved to draw and was very creative. He would gather all of us kids around a large table and have

us enter coloring contests that he found out about through a publication that listed all the contests that were going on in any month of the year. He would give us ideas and help us with our creations. As a result, we won all sorts of stuff from food coupons to cash prizes to an all train vehicle and a 95cc Harley-Davidson motorcycle.

I won three Columbia three-speed bicycles three years in a row, a rifle (like the one Lucas McCain had on the Rifleman television show) that came with 50 banana flips from the Hostess company, and a black-and-white television that Casey Jones handed over to me on one of his television shows! I won a cowboy hat, jacket, and boots in one contest. After watching an old western and seeing the cow pokes sitting around the fire with rain dripping off their hats, I went outside one rainy day and sat under the rainspout where water was draining off the roof to create the same effect on my new cowboy hat. The hat was made of felt and fell apart. I was bummed!

The whole family was once featured in a story that appeared in the Star & Tribune newspaper with all of us sitting around a table coloring our hearts out and my dad standing over us looking on with pride. I'm sure my dad's influence contributed largely to my ongoing my interest in art, my skills in drawing freehand, and willingness to jump into any creative project to see where it might lead.

Before I started kindergarten in 1962, my family moved to Southeast Minneapolis. Here I met my best friend Jay Moore. He and I grew up together in Southeast Minneapolis and were friends from preschool through our freshmen year in college. Growing up, Jay and I were like peanut butter and jelly. We were always together.

That was like Bruce and me.

Jay and I played together constantly as very young kids. We got in trouble together as older teens. We went to church together. We lived in the same neighborhood. We had the same friends. We played sports together on the same teams for baseball, football, and hockey. We earned money together working on a golf course. At one point, we even enjoyed the affections of the same girl, which caused the only source of friction I can remember in our relationship with each other.

We enjoyed a lot of activities between our two homes. We played army men on the old driveway between his house and the house that sat just north of Jay's house. We used a small rubber ball to wreak havoc on each other's army men after we strategically set them up in battle formations. It was always the Americans against the Germans and there was always a heated discussion over who was who, which we eventually settled some way or another that appeased us both. We spent hours at this game, which later developed into playing army with our friends in the hood using World War II gear that we found in Jay's garage one day. Jay's dad, Jack, was a bombardier for a flying fortress in World War II.

Sleepovers and birthday parties were never in short supply. We also shared many meals at each other's homes. I think I ate at Jay's a lot more than he ate at my house. His parents always seemed to be coming from or going to Red Owl for groceries. Jay was the second oldest of ten: three brothers and six sisters.

We built elaborate forts together in my back yard…even slept in them sometimes. Some of the forts were built halfway underground, so we could stand inside them and look out of

slats we left open to see the enemy approaching. I recall cooking cans of pork and beans over an open fire we built inside one fort. The first time we did this we smoked ourselves out because we didn't foresee having to vent the smoke to the outside.

Jay attended St. Lawrence Catholic School and I attended Tuttle Elementary School as we progressed through our elementary school years. After school and during the summer months, we were inseparable, getting into all sorts of mischief. We frequented Van Cleve Park. To us, it was a huge place where we spent most of our time. We started playing organized sports through the South East All Sports (S.E.A.S).

I taught Jay how to skate when we were eight or nine years old so we could play hockey together. He took to the game like cinnamon on buttered toast! We went out for baseball and football as well. Someplace in our elementary years, Jay moved. I think his family outgrew their house. They built a larger new home in New Brighton, Minnesota. I remember visiting them once and thinking, wow, man...you live in a mansion! The house was three stories. All the kids' rooms were on the bottom level with living areas on the middle floor and Jack and Emmy's bedroom on the top floor. They even had a tuck-under two-car garage and a dumbwaiter that went from the garage to the kitchen. The house was built on the New Brighton Golf Course, which eventually became one of Jay's favorite places to be. His dad also loved the game and made sure Jay learned how to play.

When Jay moved out of Southeast Minneapolis to New Brighton, it left a huge hole in my life. This was one of the biggest disappointments I had to handle as a young kid next to the rheumatic fever that I experienced while I was in second grade.

I remember my mom loudly telling my dad, "There's something wrong with Chris...there's something wrong with Chris!"

Hearing this at a very young age scared me and the thought that there was something wrong with me was seared into my brain. My mom diagnosed what was behind the severe pain I was experiencing in my joints and brought me to our family doctor, Dr. Bevis. She explained to the doctor what she thought I had. I was immediately sent to the hospital, where I spent the next two weeks. I learned later in life that the feeling I had that there was something wrong with me drove me to prove that there wasn't. It helped me excel in sports, but was a constant stumbling block whenever anyone criticized me or I tried to develop a serious relationship with a gal. This lie from the enemy plagued me pretty much my whole life and negatively affected all my relationships with others.

During one of our sleepovers at Jay's house, I learned that Jay had a metal plate in his head. I think the story was that he had fallen out of a window at a very young age and had to have a plate put in his head. I remember hearing that from him, thinking about it for a few seconds, and then just moving past it like it was no big deal. I don't think we ever talked about it again.

Fifth grade was a banner year. I had Mr. Hollingsworth for a teacher. He was a handsome young teacher, very athletic and built like a brick wall. He had very large hands. I learned to love geography through Mr. Hollingsworth. Mr. Hollingsworth and I both loved the game of football. One weekend he was at Van Cleve Park with the midget team he coached. He and his team were warming up on the sidelines and he was watching our game. My team was down on our one-yard line, and I was

set as a halfback in the end zone. I was given the ball on the very last play of the game and ran the ball all the way down the field for a 99-yard touchdown run to win the game for our team. Returning to school on Monday, I was so ready for him to say something about that run. The whole school day went by and he didn't even mention it. Then, as we were all lining up in the classroom to go home for the day, he said, "Oh, I almost forgot. On Saturday, I was at Van Cleve Park with the midget team I coach. I looked to the side as we were warming up and saw this little guy with his helmet bobbing up and down run the length of the field for a touchdown. That little guy was Chris Erickson. Good job, Chris!"

From my perspective, I really didn't see it that way. It was a magnificent run, fluid, graceful, and jet-burning fast... where did he get that helmet bobbling up and down stuff? Talk about ruining a moment! My first lessons about humility came through Mr. Hollingsworth.

Jay and I went through confirmation together. To prepare, those of us Catholic kids who were public schooled had to walk from Tuttle School to St. Lawrence Catholic School to attend confirmation classes. I dreaded this because I knew I would be pitted against the fastest kid in the Catholic school in an impromptu foot race after lunch during our recess time: the fastest public school runner against the fastest Catholic school runner. I couldn't eat I was so beside myself. The race started and I beat the kid I was racing hands down, much to my relief.

I did everything at Van Cleve Park.

At Sibley, I did everything as well!

Did you play chess?

Yep.

How about marbles?

Sure did.

Did you run track, wrestle, and play baseball, basketball, football, and hockey?

Yes, I did all those things plus ping-pong, horse shoes, croquet, and bait casting. I came in second place at the Sportsman Show where you had to cast rubber baits into a circle in a pool. I competed against kids from all over the city. The guy that beat me never missed a ring.

You got me on the bait casting. I did all those other things. Ok, Tom, enough. This is my childhood background we're covering.

Right, sorry.

No problem.

All my sports growing up were played through the South East All Sports. When I wasn't in school, I was down at Van Cleve Park playing whatever sport was in season. I loved football and got trophies for scoring touchdowns. Baseball was always fun as we traveled all over Minnesota to play other teams. We even played in the Stillwater State Prison. But my first love was hockey. I was definitely a rink rat, spending hours

and hours at the Van Cleve Park hockey and skating rink. Being a city park, they would flood a huge patch of ice, put up a hockey rink, and convert the park house into a warming house during the winter.

One day, I was at the rink and one of the Minnesota Gophers showed up. His name was Pete Fichuk. He put on his skates without any socks and went outside to the rink. I happened to be messing around that day and had on some goalie equipment, even though I wasn't a goalie. He asked if he could take some shots on me from the red line. I agreed and willingly got into the net. I remember bracing myself to make a save on his shot. Pete let his first shot go from the red line. I saw it come off his stick and watched it rise towards me. The puck came at me so hard and so fast, I had no time to react to it as it hit me square on the forehead and knocked me back into the net. The next thing I knew, I was inside the net with Pete apologizing and helping me get up on my skates. He and a few others helped me into the warming house. I could feel the thin, manilla mask begin to rise slowly away from my face as the bump on my forehead grew bigger and bigger. The warming house attendant looked at it and had me hold some ice on it for a few minutes. I threw the goalie equipment to the side and never wore it again. I walked home with my stick in hand and skates slid over the stick to easily carry them back. I had some explaining to do when I got home.

The South East All Sports had great uniforms and equipment for every sport. To fund the program, we sold massive amounts of candy by going in and out of all the bars in Northeast Minneapolis. Boy did those guys in the bars love candy!

The S.E.A.S provided all that we needed in green, black and white colors. One Christmas when I was in fourth grade, my aunts got together and gave me all new hockey equipment: hockey gloves, shoulder pads, and shin pads along with some warm socks. That year, I also won a coloring contest. The prize was a $50 gift certificate that was good for purchasing sporting equipment at ABC Sports in downtown Minneapolis. With that $50 certificate, I bought my first pair of brand new skates and a hockey stick. The skates had the brand name "Bauer" on the back in gold letters and provided some support I never knew you needed.

I used those skates until my sophomore year in high school. The blades had been sharpened so many times they were almost down to nothing and the toes were so soft that any time I got dinged with a puck it would send me writhing in pain. Eventually, I could hold the skates up by the blades and the boots on each skate would simply fall sideways. No support whatsoever! My coaches through the years could not figure out how I could skate the way I did in those skates, given their condition. I didn't know any better. It's what I had, and I made them work and did things on the ice that made me feel like I was flying!

I played football for the District III South East All Sports Cubs team even though I was a peewee. It was a squad of 32 players and my brother Jeff was on the team. All my best friends were on the peewee team, but I was playing with all the guys I knew through my brother or hung out with in the neighborhood. This was a talented team and filled with personality, every one of them. I eventually went back down to the peewee team because I missed playing with all of my friends.

The thing I remember most fondly about playing sports at Van Cleve Park is my dad, who would always make time to come watch me play. It didn't matter which sport or what time of year it was. He would be standing off to the side someplace in sunshine or rainy weather or frigid cold temperatures. My dad smoked a pipe. Anytime I wanted to pinpoint his location, I simply scanned the line of parents and stopped when I saw some smoke lingering in the air just above the parents' heads. There was my dad, pipe in hand as he puffed away.

We moved again, this time from Minneapolis out to New Brighton, after I completed seventh grade at Marshall University High School. Even though my family moved out to the northern suburb of New Brighton from Southeast Minneapolis, I continued to play sports with the S.E.A.S. We had winning teams, and I had a hard time letting go of my involvement in this program.

When winter hit, I could no longer ride my bike into Minneapolis from New Brighton, so my playing days with the S.E.A.S came to an end and I focused my attention on hockey in the Lake Region Youth Hockey Association. I had to break into a new league without a reputation or the top-of-the-line equipment that the suburban kids had. I went to the bantam tryouts, never having been to a tryout before. Those in charge had us do a bunch of drills I was not familiar with. My skates were mistakenly sharpened flat instead of hollow which really caused me some concern, especially on my old skates. I missed making the Bantam A team by one point and ended up playing Bantam B hockey, which turned out to be a lot of fun. Hockey was my sport!

Leaving our home in Minneapolis and ending my days playing for the S.E.A.S also meant having to make new friends. The tension between making new friends and doing what those new friends are doing is always a difficult thing to navigate. As a result, I started drinking in seventh grade and continued drinking into eighth grade at my new school in New Brighton. My drinking habits steadily got worse through ninth grade. Through junior high, there were three girls I liked, but one really stood out to me towards the end of ninth grade. That's the relationship I pursued off and on through high school and into college. I continued to be influenced by serious partying and smoking pot, of which Tom probably had no knowledge. Tom continued to see something in me I did not see. He faithfully prayed for me and was as purposeful in developing a friendship with me as I was with him.

Roosevelt High School

As Bruce and I got older, our friendship changed. He matured a little sooner than I did. He started drinking, smoking, and going to parties. I didn't quite fit in anymore. However, sports kept our friendship going. In our junior year in high school, our varsity hockey team went to the state tournament, which is a big deal in Minnesota. Bruce and I roomed together at the Saint Paul Hotel. It was like a dream come true for both of us. We lost in the first game in three overtimes. However, we went on to win the state consolation championship. It was a memory that both of us will never forget.

It's funny, but I never even thought of the state tournament when I played hockey. Maybe because I only played high school hockey during my sophomore year. My mom was very surprised when I bought an Irondale letterman's jacket and then never put anything on it, even though I lettered in three sports and was a captain for one. I just loved to play. I really didn't care about all the peripheral stuff.

In the summer of our senior year, Bruce was caught drinking at a party. He was not allowed to participate in any sports his senior year. That was difficult for him because sports were his life. He would have lettered in football, hockey, and baseball. He was crushed and I really felt bad for him. We needed him on our hockey team because he was a great scorer. I didn't see much of Bruce all that year.

I think Bruce and I had some common experiences, but maybe caused by different things. I would venture to say that the empathy you felt towards me might have been born out of your experiences with Bruce.

You're quite the counselor, Chris.

Our hockey team did really well my senior year. I was the leading scorer in the city. We won the city championship. Then, we lost a game in the regional finals in a very close match that kept us from going to the state tournament. I was very disappointed. I felt that if our team had done better, I could have gotten a hockey scholarship. That never happened. I believe I had good talent, but never realized my goals as a hockey player. But I had a very good year playing hockey, and at the end of the season, I was named first line center on the All-City squad.

Tom, you were a better hockey player than I was. Maybe not as fast, but wiser and craftier than me.

At church, I met a lovely young girl named Sandy. She was two and a half years younger than me. I was always nervous and uncomfortable around girls.

Not me!

I asked my younger brother Bob to test the waters. He talked to Sandy and asked her if she would be interested in going out with me, his older brother. She indicated that she was interested. I didn't know if she even knew me! I was very nervous when I called her and asked her to go on a date with me. When she said yes, I hung up the phone and was filled with joy. That relationship would drastically impact my life.

After graduating from high school with no hockey scholarship, I had to work for a year to help my mother out financially. This was difficult for me since all of my friends were at college. My older brother and sister got married, so I was the oldest one at home. I had a lot of responsibility and had trouble handling the load.

Sandy

After working for a year, I enrolled at the University of Minnesota. My motivation was to play hockey and get an education on the side. My dream was to play hockey for the Golden Gophers. I tried out for and made the freshman team. In those days the freshmen were not allowed to play varsity hockey. I did very well playing for the freshman team and had a good shot at making the varsity the next year, but I had to drop out of college and work because I didn't have enough money to continue my education.

Where did you work?

I worked at the University Hospital on the weekends for ten hours each day. My weekend seemed so long that I was glad to get back to my college classes on Monday. In the summer, I worked at a trucking company loading and unloading trucks and made pretty good money.

One time while working at this trucking company, I was given the assignment to unload a forty-foot trailer. I was on a night shift from 11 p.m. until 7 a.m. When I cracked the seal and opened the truck, the stench almost knocked me over. I looked at the chart in my hand and saw that this truck was filled with fifty-pound bags of dried chicken blood. I wondered why anyone would want dried chicken blood! It was a hot evening and I was already sweating before I started. I had to pick up these bags by hand and put them on a palate. When I was partway through, I thought I was going to die from the heat and the smell. I picked up another bag and it broke, sending dried chicken blood all over me. Just then, a friend saw me struggling and wanted to help me. After he and I filled another palate, he apologized and said he couldn't help me anymore because he couldn't stand the smell. I thanked him for the effort and was determined to get the rest of the truck unloaded. Halfway through, I went to the break room for a rest and a snack. I smelled so bad that everyone left the room! After many hours, I finally saw the back of the truck and knew I could complete it! It was the hardest thing I've ever done in my life.

Tom, I knew you were strong, but I didn't know you were that shy! You should've asked for help! Great story. It reminds me of a time in Albania with an EPPIC crew when we were tasked with separating moldy cheese from food packs stored in a hot and humid metal warehouse.

Hey, did you ever play varsity hockey at the University of Minnesota?

At that time, I was in a serious relationship with Sandy. She was also in college. When I returned to college as a sophomore in 1963, I still wanted to fulfill my dream of playing hockey for the Golden Gophers. However, I was not a good student and getting an education would take my full effort. Hockey became secondary and my new goal was to graduate with a degree in education. My dream of playing hockey for the Gophers never came true.

One winter night, I drove by Sibley Park. I parked my car, grabbed my skates, stick, and puck, and headed for the rink. There was no one else there, just me and the rink illuminated by a streetlight. I skated around the rink shooting and stick handling the puck. I skated until I was completely exhausted. I laid flat on my back on the ice, looking up at the stars. I remembered all the goals scored, the excitement of the crowds, and the thrill of the game. I was grateful for hockey because it gave me status and it helped my self-esteem, but it was time to move on. I took off my skates, headed back to the car and decided to put hockey on the back burner in my life. It wouldn't dominate me anymore. Before, I had lived for hockey. Now, I needed to move on and get an education.

Where did Sandy go to college?

Sandy was going to Bethel College at the time. When we talked about getting married, she said she could get a full-time job, and I could carry on with my education and work part-time. She convinced me it was possible for us to get married.

On one occasion while we were dating, Sandy asked me to go "shoe shopping" with her. She conveniently walked us by a jewelry store. She turned to me and said, "Tom,

I know you're not ready for this, but if you ever consider marrying me, that's the ring I want," and pointed to a beautiful diamond ring in the glass display. That comment made me think about marriage for the first time. I decided right there I had found the one I wanted to marry.

Soon after, I went back to that jewelry store and asked them if they could put the ring on hold. I was working at Donaldson's Warehouse at the time and was able to eventually save up enough to buy the ring for Sandy. I hid the ring in my bedroom for several weeks. She had impressed on me that if I was ever interested in marrying her, I would need to ask her dad first. I was kind of afraid of him, to be honest. He was very protective of his daughter.

You must have been pretty sure of yourself by buying the ring even before asking him for his daughter's hand in marriage.

One evening, I got up my courage to go to Sandy's house to speak with her parents when I knew she would not be home. I rang the doorbell and her mother answered. She said, "Hi Tom! Sandy's not here right now."

"I came to talk to your husband," I responded.

"He's out in the garage working on his car," she told me. I walked into the garage and found him laying down under his car, fixing something. I stood there for a long time before I said anything. Eventually I said, "Mr. Johnson, can I talk to you?"

He rolled out from under the car and looked at me. He was covered in grease and oil.

"What can I do for you?" he asked.

"It's about your daughter."

"Yes?"

"I'd like your permission for her hand in marriage," I said. There was a long pause. It was agonizing.

"We won't get married right away; it will be a little while."

"Let me get cleaned up, then we'll go inside to talk with the missus."

He got cleaned up while Mrs. Johnson prepared coffee and a little treat. We sat down at the kitchen table. After some small talk, Mr. Johnson turned to his wife and said, "Tom has asked my permission for Sandy's hand in marriage." Mrs. Johnson got all excited.

"That's great, Tom! When are you planning on asking her?"

"I couldn't ask her until I talked to you. She made that very clear," I replied.

A few weeks later, in the spring of 1963, we went out for pizza at a nice place called Italian Village. I had the ring in my pocket the whole time. She didn't know that I had talked to her parents. As we were driving home, I pulled over on a side street and parked the car. "What are you doing?" she asked.

"Do you love me?" I asked her.

"Yes, you know I love you!" she responded, a bit confused.

"No, I mean really love, like…forever?"

"Why are you asking me these questions?" Sandy cried. I had the ring in my hand and tried to slip it on her finger while she was talking. "That's the wrong hand!" she exclaimed as she started crying.

"Will you marry me?" I asked as I put the ring on the correct hand.

"Yes! Have you talked to my parents?"

"Of course I have!" We drove back to her house and showed her parents the ring. Everyone was excited.

Her mom's support throughout our relationship really encouraged me as I felt I didn't have much to offer. She saw potential in me that I didn't see in myself.

Where did Sandy work while you were in school?

She got a very good job at the Minneapolis Gas Company. We were able to make it financially while I finished my education.

Sandy and I got married on September 7th,1963. She was 19 and I had just turned 22.

Now that we were married, I was motivated to work hard on my studies. I don't believe I would've graduated without Sandy's help and encouragement. I graduated in 1966 with a teaching degree and got a teaching position in California that same year.

I've come to know and love Sandy. You are so blessed to have met her early and married her. She's a gem!

I didn't realize it at the time, but next to receiving Jesus as my personal Savior, that was the best decision I have ever made! She is beautiful, intelligent, and godly. We have very different personalities. She's an introvert; I'm an extrovert. She is organized and has great attention to detail; I'm a little more random and big-picture oriented. God said that when two get married, they become one. Through our 57 years of marriage, we have become a great team. God has used Sandy in my life in an incredible way. So many times throughout our marriage, she has pushed me to Christ and helped me grow in huge ways. I'm so thankful for her.

I have thoroughly enjoyed witnessing your amazing relationship with Sandy over the years. It amuses me to no end, watching and listening to her hold you accountable for the random things you do. I'm smiling now just thinking about it!

California

Sandy and I packed everything we had and moved to California in the summer of 1966.

Did you drive to California?

Yes, in our new 1966 Chevy Impala two-door hard top with a 396 engine!

How was the trip?

I was sad to leave Minneapolis for the first time in my life. As I drove out of the city, I looked back and wondered if we would ever return. I was leaving my family behind. It was a good trip in our new car, and we were excited when we drove into Los Angeles. I had a friend named Bob Larson who was teaching at the high school in Palos Verdes. He arranged for us to have an apartment when we arrived. We only paid $85 a month and it was two blocks off the ocean. It was so close we could hear the waves pounding against the shore in the evenings.

For people from Minnesota, the weather was incredible! However, during my third year in California, I saw a movie about Christmas and it really made me miss the white Christmas I was used to enjoying.

I taught at Vista Grande Elementary School in Palos Verdes, California. This was a suburb of Los Angeles located on the ocean. I could see the ocean from the window in my classroom. Sometimes, we even saw the whales migrating south and blowing water up into the air. It was cool for a city boy who had never seen the ocean! It was at this school where I met Bill Spivey. I owe my career to him.

In California, I really struggled teaching. I was miserable and didn't think I would make it through the first year. Fortunately, God came through and helped me out. Bill Spivey and I began our careers together and became lifelong friends. We were like ketchup and mustard, different but always together.

Are you still good friends with Bill? Where's he living now?

Bill is now retired and is living in Salem, Oregon. We're still good friends!

In California, Bill helped me develop my own teaching style.

How did he do that?

He led by example and was willing to tell me the truth. At the start of our very first school year, Bill was more confident than I was and did a great job right out of the chute.

His kids loved him, whereas my kids had trouble with me because I was so strict. I had been told by my student teaching supervisor at the University of Minnesota that if I smiled before Christmas, the kids would not respect me. Bill's teaching style flatly contradicted that advice. As I watched Bill teach, I was amazed at how much fun he was having and how much his kids respected him. Everyone was smiling in his classroom!

One time, we were in the car driving to Long Beach College to work on our master's degrees. I turned to Bill and asked him, "How do you do it?"

Confused, Bill asked me what I meant. I proceeded to ask him how he could teach his kids and have so much fun while I felt like I was dying.

"Do you want the truth?" he asked.

"Straight up!"

"I know the guy sitting next to me in the car, but I don't know the guy up there in front of the class!"

"What do you mean?"

Bill explained to me that the kids had to see who I really was, not who I thought I should be. He encouraged me to let my personality come out and have fun while teaching. By the end of the year, I was doing much better. After three years, I fell in love with teaching and decided it would be my lifetime career.

Did you look for a church out there?

As a matter of fact, we did. It was a big adjustment for Sandy and me to move to a place where we didn't know anyone. I got really homesick. We knew we needed to find a church family. Sandy wanted to go to a General Conference Baptist Church like we did back home. She found one in Torrance, California about fifteen minutes away. One Sunday, we decided to try it out and arrived a little late. As we walked in, we saw about eight people in the pews and one guy up in the pulpit reading Scripture with a thick accent. Thinking it was the wrong church, we turned around and walked out. Before we got to our car, several of them came running after us and asked us why we were leaving. We said that we were looking for the General Conference Baptist Church.

"That's who we are! Come on back!" they said.

This church turned out to be an incredible home away from home for Sandy and me. We became very involved and quite close to many amazing couples. We were all recently married and didn't have kids yet, which allowed us to spend a significant amount of time together and have a lot of freedom. We even had a church softball and basketball team. It was a blast!

The church grew to about two hundred people by the time we left. It was really hard to leave this church after attending for three years. God used this body of believers to reignite my faith and strengthen my marriage. I'm really thankful for the years we spent in California.

Back to Minnesota

I called my brother Dave from California and asked him if he could get me an interview at the school district in which he worked. He said he would check it out. Dave called back the next day and said, "There's a contract in the mail." I asked him how I could get a job without an interview. He replied, "It's networking." Dave knew the person who was hiring teachers in that district and told him that his brother Tom was teaching in California and had three years under his belt. Dave told him I was athletic and loved kids. Apparently, his friend responded, "That's all I need to know!" and decided to send me a contract. Sandy and I moved back to Minnesota, and I secured a teaching position in the Mounds View School District.

Networking was still in play when I interviewed for my first teaching position. I talked with a principal in Rogers, Minnesota. He wanted to hire me, but had already filled his third through sixth grade positions. He floated my name to Bob Hallet, the principal at Forest Hills Elementary School in Eden Prairie, Minnesota. Bob hired me to fill two long-term sub positions in 5th grade, which turned into another long-term

sub position for a year and eventually led to a full-time position which I enjoyed for 15 years, all at Forest Hills. God was at work providing me with employment.

I had three years under my belt and realized I could relate to my students and win their respect. If I hadn't started my first job in California and hadn't met Bill Spivey, my career would have been short-lived. God wanted me in education, and part of his plan involved three years in California for Sandy and me.

And I got into education because of your influence in my life. God was at work there too!

For me, I always looked forward to going to work because no two days were the same. I loved my students and became passionate about my career. Being a Christian teacher in the public school proved to be a great ministry. I had the word of God as my standard and the Holy Spirit as my guide. I would shoot up prayers all day long which helped me problem solve and reach difficult students. I have had the fortunate experience to share the gospel message with former students. Chris, you are an example of one of those students, although I never taught you in a classroom setting.

That was my loss...or maybe your good fortune!

When Sandy and I moved back to Minnesota, we lived in an apartment for a year. Mike, our firstborn son, came when we were living in that apartment. He was born January 1st on a cold, wintery morning. Sandy went into the hospital on December 30th. We were hoping our son would be born before the new year. We were poor and needed a tax break! Mike, however, took his own sweet time. As it turned out, eight other babies were born in the hospital before my son came. In those days, the fathers would stay in a waiting room anticipating the good news that their child was born.

When each of my daughters were born, I was in the room and witnessed their births. Each birth was a miraculous event and an amazing experience for me.

When the nurse came in, we all jumped up expecting to be the lucky new dad. After a while, I didn't jump any more. Finally, after 38 hours, I became extremely frightened and was concerned for Sandy's life. I prayed, "Please God, take care of my wife. Help her be safe! Don't make me choose between my child and my wife." While I was praying, a doctor came into the waiting room. I got scared as I listened for what the doctor had to say.

"Your wife is not opening up enough for this baby to be born, and she is quite weak. We need to do a cesarean section operation," he said. I wasn't quite sure what that was, so I asked him to explain what that meant. "We need to open her up to remove the baby," the doctor explained. "She will have a longer recovery time, but she will heal up and be fine. We need your permission to be able to proceed." I then asked him if we would be able to have more children after such a procedure. He assured me that we could definitely have more kids. I gave my consent and they proceeded with the surgery.

When the doctor left, I was exhausted. I hadn't slept for a long time and was very concerned for the health of my wife.

The next day, the other fathers came back to see their newborn babies. They were surprised to find me still in the waiting room. They had many questions. I felt these men knew me and were concerned because my child hadn't come yet. Finally, I heard my name and came to the window and saw my son for the first time. He looked perfect because he didn't have to struggle through the birth canal. A nurse was holding up my son so I could see his entire body. Suddenly he had a bowl movement. I made a face, but she just smiled at me. Then, she laid our baby down, cleaned him up, and came out to visit me. "Congratulations! You have a beautiful son!"

I thanked her for taking care of my son and went to see Sandy. I walked into her room where she was lying down. She looked tired and turned towards me as I approached her bed. "Hi babe! Thank you for our son!" I said as I bent down and kissed her tenderly on her forehead.

A nurse came in and gently handed me Michael, and I cradled him in my arms for the first time. He was so small and delicate. I loved him with everything I had. It was a moment in my life that I will never forget. I was a father! My life was about to change forever.

I felt the same way when my daughter Christina was born. Looking down onto the meandering Mississippi River from my wife's hospital room, I was overwhelmed with an awesome sense of responsibility. It scared me to the point of doubting whether I could handle that responsibility or not. Then a still small voice within me seemed to say, "It's okay. You'll be fine. You can do all things through Christ who strengthens you." A tremendous sense of peace and joy flooded over me, giving me the confidence I needed.

I left Sandy and my son and drove home. I was so tired I barely made it home. I had trouble keeping my eyes open. At one moment, my eyes shut and as they opened again, I was off the road heading for a tree. I quickly turned and just barely missed the tree. When I finally got home and hit the bed, I fell asleep instantaneously as my head hit the pillow.

Things have improved! I was able to stay with my wife in the hospital for a few days and didn't have to go home or teach as we went through the birth of our firstborn.

Almost two years later, Katie was born. She was another precious gift from the Lord! In 1972, we were a family of four. We moved out of our apartment into a small two-bedroom home in Brooklyn Center, which is a suburb in North Minneapolis. Sandy and I have lived there ever since. It was a good school district for our kids and a great place for Mike and Katie to grow and develop. God is good!

Sandy and I had not found a church in Minnesota yet. We had a great experience in the small church in California, so we tried to find a similar church. We went for three years in Minnesota without a church family in our lives, which was not good. Sandy suggested we try the Christian Missionary Alliance Church just one block from our home. I knew that for the kids' sake, we needed to be involved in a local church. The impact this church had on the life of our family was tremendous.

Northbrook Alliance Church was a wonderful choice. Their theology was quite similar to the church in which Sandy and I grew up. They had a solid Sunday school program for young children. The church had a great pastor who delivered excellent sermons each Sunday. We attended a young adults Sunday school class with many adults our age who also had small children. The people that directed the young adults class were outstanding role models for us as young parents. We were very close to about five couples. We held a Bible study in our home, which was helpful in raising young children. This study met every other Friday, and our group had great fellowship with each other for a couple of years.

Our children began to grow, which required a lot of attention from both of us. Sandy was a wonderful mother! She set the limits and disciplined the children when they crossed the line. When I came home from work, the children always greeted me with hugs and smiles. I would wrestle with them on the floor every day. I loved being with them! As they grew older, I realized I couldn't treat my daughter the same way I treated my son. She was a little girl and I needed to treat her gently with love and respect. With Mike, I could roughhouse a little bit more, and he loved it.

I enjoyed my job very much. My three years of experience in California helped me to be the teacher I wanted to be. I was confident and able to focus on my students. I wanted to give them a year that they would never forget. I used illustrations and stories from my own life to keep their interest. I taught about values and character qualities that they could use as adults. I wanted the atmosphere in my room to be a place where students could thrive. I wanted them to know that the things they learned in my classroom would help them throughout their lives. A lot of Bill Spivey rubbed off on me. My new career and church helped us mature and grow as a family.

The Cardiologist

Going into tenth grade, I had to have a high school physical in order to play sports. When I went in to see my family physician in August 1972, my doctor sent me to a cardiologist. It was there at the cardiologist's office that I was informed that I had a condition called post-rheumatic valvular insufficiency with mild associated aortic stenosis, well compensated, functional class I. I called it "aortic insufficiency." Because of this condition, I was very heavily cautioned not to play sports, but was given an "okay" to do so with limitations.

I played sophomore football because the sophomore football coach knew me from summer football. I quarterbacked the summer team his son was playing on and that he was coaching. Coach Klitzke played me at quarterback, but because of my heart condition he would never let me run the ball. On the very last play of the season, he let me run. I can still feel the play to this day. I got the ball, broke through the line, totally faked a linebacker out of his shorts, cut right towards the sidelines, ran for about 30 yards and then went head on with the safety of the opposing team. In those days there were not any rules against that kind of play. We hit so hard that my head was spinning when I got up from the ground (that's why they have the rules now). This became the very last play of my football days and it felt great! Holding back all year only served to make me push forward more, vainly trying to prove there was nothing wrong with me or my heart.

Then Dave Hall, Tom's older brother, brought me onto the varsity hockey team. Coach Hall knew about my heart condition and let me play anyway. I was one of only two sophomores who joined the team of upperclassmen. I respected Coach Hall for this. He didn't place any restrictions on me and treated me just like all the other players. Mr. Hall was also the teacher who took me out into the hallway one morning, threw me up against the wall, and spoke truth to me about my poor attitude towards school. He warned me that I had better shape up. There's something to be said about how disciplining a student can often create respect rather than animosity.

The varsity hockey team that Dave Hall coached was a hard group of guys. They were a crazy bunch who drank and smoked pot. My exposure to this crowd brought me into a lot of things I probably wouldn't have done on my own as a sophomore. On a hockey trip up north, some of the guys on the team were drinking and smoking pot on the bus. The word got out about this unfortunate incident, and eventually school officials heard about it. Coach Hall ended up taking responsibility for his team's behavior and did not return to coach the following year. At the end of the year, Coach Hall wrote in my year book:

"Chris, good luck with hockey next year. Pass the puck often and get a lot of rebounds and goals. Dave Hall."

Chris, we both have had my older brother Dave as our hockey coach at some point in our lives. That's another commonality between us! My brother Dave drummed into my head to pass the puck to the open man. He wanted me to realize that hockey was a team sport. Dave wanted me to be an unselfish player, so that was the way I played. My teammates knew that if they were open, I would give them the puck. Therefore, they did not hesitate to give it back to me when I was open. They trusted me to carry it and get us in scoring position.

I'm thankful for your brother Dave. In the short time that I knew him, he taught me a lot.

I played baseball during this same school year and the doctors were not at all concerned with me playing this sport. However, I think the knowledge of my heart condition put me on edge and unknowingly forced me to want to perform better. I also got into a lot of fights both on and off the field. I think this is how I was dealing with my heart condition and trying to prove it wasn't there. My behavior only fed the lie I was unknowingly believing about myself that there was something wrong with me.

A Summer School Course

During my fourth year teaching in Minnesota, one of my colleagues asked me to join him and another teacher for a little discussion. So I got together with our gym teacher Jim and a sixth-grade teacher named John during lunch.

"Have you ever been to the Boundary Waters in Northern Minnesota?'" asked John with a smile on his face.

"Not really, but I've camped on the Sawbill Trail, which is similar. Why do you ask?" I responded.

"Our district is encouraging teachers to write creative summer school courses. John and I were considering taking students on a seven-day camping trip to the Boundary Waters. I have a good friend who has an outfitting business and can set us up with canoes and tents. It would be a wonderful trip for kids to experience this incredible environment," explained Jim.

"Wouldn't it take a lot of work to write a program that extensive?" I questioned.

"We thought if the three of us could put our heads together, we could write a curriculum filled with goals and objectives for students to experience in the wilderness," John told me.

"We would spend a week preparing the students for this adventure. We could teach them how to paddle a canoe, set up a tent, and cook over an open fire," explained Jim.

"I have a friend who has a home on Long Lake. We could use his property and the lake to train the students for this experience. It will not be a picnic. We will have to get them ready both physically and mentally," explained John.

"Why are you asking me?" I questioned.

"We thought you might be interested because you love the outdoors," commented John.

"Also, you really love kids and would be a great asset to our team," threw in Jim.

"What do you say, Hallsey? Does this seem like something you would be interested in?"

"Yeah, I'm interested! But I have young kids at home and it might be kind of tough leaving Sandy alone with them for a couple of weeks. You did say we would be taking two trips during the summer, didn't you?"

"Yes. However, we would get paid the summer school rate and have a great time doing it," stated John.

"Wow! You guys are thinking big! I like what I'm hearing. But don't hold your breath. It's kind of a long shot that Sandy will go for it. I would love to be a part of this project, so I'll try my best to convince my wife. I'll let you guys know my answer on Monday."

That weekend, I waited for a good time to pop the question to my wife since I knew there would be some discussion before I got Sandy's approval. On Saturday night after the kids were in bed, we were sitting in our living room.

"You know I have to get a summer job." I threw my comment out there like I was fishing.

"Have you thought about a place to get a job yet?" A little nibble.

"I had an offer this week in school." Get ready to set the hook.

"What kind of an offer was it?" Patience.

"Jim Sorteberg and John Jones are writing a summer school course and asked if I wanted to be included."

"What kind of a course is it?" Patience.

"It involves writing up a creative summer school course as an enrichment class."

"How creative is it?" Easy now. Tease that fishing line a little more.

"They want to take junior high students on a seven-day camping trip into the Boundary Waters Canoe Area up north." Boom! Set the hook.

"Wow! That's very creative."

"It would mean that I would be away for 14 days." Start reeling in the line.

"Are you interested?"

"Very!" Steady.

"Have you thought this through? That's a huge responsibility! What if something terrible happened?" Steady. Keep the line taut.

"We would be employed by the school district, so I think there would be insurance of some kind. I would hate to leave you alone with the kids for two weeks this summer. However, the pay is pretty good, and I wouldn't be gone all summer."

"I don't know Tom. That seems like too big of a risk." Let out the line a bit.

"It'll be fine. I was just worried about you and the kids."

"You really want to do this, don't you?" Careful now. Reel slowly.

"Yes!"

"Well, I think it might work. I could have my mother stay with us and she would love it," Sandy responded.

"Is that a yes?"

"Yes, it is, Tommy. But promise me you will be careful with all those kids in the wilderness."

"I promise." That's a catch!

The following Monday, I sat down with Jim and John during our lunch hour. They were both curious about my answer.

"Well Tom, did you talk to your wife?"

"I did. We had a long discussion. She thought it was quite a risk taking junior high kids that you don't know into the wilderness." I smirked, stringing my colleagues along a little bit.

"What's your decision?" asked Jim.

"She gave me the green light!" I replied triumphantly. A big smile broke out over both Jim's and John's faces. The summer school course was on! We started writing the curriculum the very next day. This course, which we taught for several summers, would eventually bring Chris into my path and spark the beginning of a lifelong friendship.

Growing Inside, Outside

The summer of 1973 proved to be a pivotal time in my life. During this time, I met Tom Hall. I also discovered another outlet to appease my frustration regarding my heart condition.

"Hey Chris, can I talk to you?" my sister Jane yelled from upstairs.

"What do you want? I'm heading out," I replied.

"I wanted to ask if you would be a part of a summer school class I'm taking at High View Junior High School with some of my friends."

"What? No way. I have no desire to spend any of my summer with junior highers!" I responded ungraciously.

"Come on, Chris. It will be fun! It's a wilderness canoe camping program that a few elementary teachers are offering through the Mounds View School District," she wheedled with a pleasantly playful tone. "We need more people to sign up! We'll be going to the Boundary Waters Canoe Area."

"Wait a minute. Wilderness canoe camping? Boundary Waters Canoe Area?" I questioned. "Sounds interesting... where's this Boundary Waters anyway?" I asked.

"It's called the Boundary Waters Canoe Area, or BWCA for short. It's in northern Minnesota and crosses over into Canada," she informed me.

"Who's going?" I asked.

"Well, I know Kris Larson and Kathy Thomas are going, along with some other kids I don't know."

"Really?" I replied nonchalantly. "When's the trip?"

Jane successfully baited me into signing up for the summer school course by mentioning the names of a few girls I knew. Later in the week, we entered a pod-type classroom at High View Junior High outside of the main building.

That sounds like you, Chris. You needed the motivation of some cute girls to get you to go on the trip!

No comment.

As soon as I entered the door, Tom and I caught a glimpse of each other, and I immediately felt a connection to this man. In that instant, through a simple moment of eye contact, the beginning of an extraordinary relationship took root.

The title of the wilderness canoe camping program in the summer of 1973 was "Growing Inside, Outside." The title was very appropriate for everything going on in my life and Tom's life over the five years that Tom and his colleagues taught the course. Our relationship grew as we explored the wilderness together as campers in the BWCA.

At the beginning of my third year teaching the summer program, I met Chris. He was an interesting young man with so much potential. When I met him, I already had two trips with students to the BWCA under my belt. I had some experience with how the course should run, and the program was laid out and running smoothly before Chris entered the picture. My colleagues and I worked well together and shared the load of all the work involved. We each had our roles to play and took turns with our presentations during the first meeting. As the students walked into our classroom, I noticed Chris right away. We made eye contact and he gave me a confident smile. At the end of our first meeting, we divided the students into three groups. Each group would then travel through the rest of the training together and compete against each other in a fun way throughout the course of the week. I wanted Chris to be in my group and convinced Jim and John to grant me that favor.

We trained the kids for a week and got them ready for a trip to the Boundary Waters. They all learned how to paddle a canoe, set up a tent, and cook over an open fire in the back yard of Jim's friend's house on Long Lake. We also did some rigorous exercises to get them ready for the long paddles and portages they would have to conquer on this trip.

Remember when Sorteberg challenged me to a push-up contest? I think I did like 75 of them, but he easily blew my record and explained later that he did 150 push-ups every morning! That was a humbling experience. He was solid and built like a brick wall.

After the three groups went through all the training, each leader would take their group on a seven-day canoe camping trip. Each group planned out a different route in the beautiful wilderness of the BWCA.

This is when I started journaling. I secured two tiny spiral-bound notepads and began writing.

The bus ride to our destination was about a four-hour journey. I made a point to sit with each of the students in my group at some point during the ride to get to know them better. I would answer any questions that they might have. I wanted them to know I had been on a few trips and they could trust me to take good care of them. Chris was sitting next to a girl as I approached him.

"Can I have a few words with you, Chris?" I asked politely.

"Well, I'm a little busy right now," responded Chris.

"Go ahead, Mr. Hall. I'll catch you later, Chris," said the girl sitting by him as she glanced at him with a twinkle in her eye.

"How are you doing, Chris?" I asked.

"I'm excited! It should be quite an adventure," he responded. I wanted to get his story, so I began to probe.

"Are you going to be a sophomore this year?"

"No, actually I'll be a junior."

"Where are you going to school?"

"Irondale," he replied quickly.

"My brother teaches there. He's also the hockey coach. His name is Dave Hall. You probably know him as Mr. Hall or Coach Hall I guess."

"Really? I played varsity last year. So, Davey-boy is your brother! It's a small world! He's a great coach even though our record was 3 and 19. I'm looking forward to this coming season. I really respect your brother. Last year, he literally called me out into the hall and threw me up against the wall and read me the riot act."

"Why did he do that?" I asked.

"I was goofing around in his electronics class. I had it coming."

"I come from a hockey family. All my brothers play. Maybe that's something we have in common."

As we talked, I noticed that Chris was a confident young man who loved life and was ready to experience all life had in its fullness. I was glad he was in my group. Something special took place on that bus as Chris and I began a mutual friendship that has not only lasted a lifetime, but will last into eternity as well.

When we got to the outfitters, we gathered together in our separate groups. The students had to find a partner and pack in pairs. Chris packed with a girl who we nicknamed Flossie because her dad was a dentist and she was always flossing her beautiful pearly white teeth. Two campers' necessities had to fit into one Duluth Pack.

I remember packing with Floss. I was always teasing her. I think we had an uneven number of guys and gals on the trip, so

someone had to share a pack with a girl. I think I volunteered the two of us for the chore.

I pulled Chris aside. "This will be a great experience for us, but it will not be a picnic. There will be some rough times and I will need your help and depend on your leadership skills. Can I count on you?"

"Yeah, Mr. Hall. I got your back!"

"It's not Mr. Hall anymore on this trip. You can call me Hallsey."

"Hallsey it is!"

We loaded our canoes and pushed off. I was in the stern of one of the canoes and Chris was in the stern of another. We needed our strongest paddlers in the stern. We had eight students on this trip, five boys and three girls. A colleague of mine also came along to help chaperone the girls. Her name was Kris, but we called her Red because her skin turned red in the sun's rays and she had strawberry blonde hair. Kris and I taught together at Pike Lake School.

As we launched the canoes, Chris bellowed, "Yahoo! Let's get this show on the road! Or should I say, on the water!"

I knew Chris would be a great asset on this trip. My plans for our group included cliff diving, swimming in the cool waters, fishing, and singing around our campfires. I wanted us to become a closely-knit family for the duration of the trip, but I knew it would take some time.

On our first day, we paddled out of the channel, made a left turn, and entered a wide expanse of water called

Lake Saganaga. We were searching for our first campsite on American Point. We stopped and pulled our canoes onto a small island after a long paddle. Marian, one of the students in our group, stepped on a sharp rock and severely cut her foot. I was sure she needed stitches. We were going to paddle back to the outfitters and have a doctor look after Marian's wound, but spotted a boat with a motor and hailed him to our island. As he came closer, it was clear that he was a forest ranger because of the logo on his boat.

"What's the matter?" the ranger asked.

"We have an injury. Can you help us?"

Without saying a word, he swiftly came ashore.

"My name is Tom Hall. I'm the leader of this group. One of my students stepped on a sharp rock and cut her foot," I explained.

"Let me see the cut."

Marian was sitting on a rock. She was a brave girl and toughing it out. I pulled off her stocking and removed the bandages.

He looked at her foot and said, "That's deep. It's going to require stitches."

"I think we have to return to our outfitters and have a doctor take care of that wound," I said to the ranger.

"You don't have to do that. I can take her back in my boat. What's the name of your outfitter?"

"Saganaga Outfitters...the Germains," I blurted out.

"I know Don personally. Here's what I suggest. I'll take her back and get her fixed up and bring her back in the morning. Where are you going to settle for the night?"

"We're heading for American Point."

"I know exactly where that is," he said as he pointed off to the left at an angle. "You see that point over there? Once you get inside that narrows, you'll find two campsites. The first one is better than the second. There's a picnic table and a latrine at the first site. It should provide you with everything you need. Wait for us in the morning and we'll meet up with you then."

Calmly, I looked into Marian's eyes and asked, "How does that sound, Marian?"

"That sounds great! I thought for sure my camping trip was over."

"Goodbye, then. We'll see you in the morning," I said.

All the students gathered around and gave her further encouragement. I turned to the ranger and asked him his name.

"Joe," he informed me with a smile.

"Joe, I really appreciate your kindness. You have gone above and beyond."

"You're welcome, Tom. I think everything will work out for the best."

I smiled, picked Marian up, and gently placed her on the middle bench in the ranger's boat.

He climbed into his boat and backed out into the bay. Waving, he turned about and sped across Saganaga heading toward the channel leading to the Germaines' place.

"Everybody up here," Red summoned.

One of the canoes was turned over and being used as a table. Red and one of the girls named Sandy had made cheese sandwiches. In addition, they had put trail mix in cups and mixed up a gallon of Orange Wylers. Everyone was hungry because of all the paddling that morning. The waters of Lake Saganaga were making their presence known by showing their white teeth as gusts of wind whipped up frothy waves of water.

"It's getting pretty rough out there," stated Chris.

"It sure is. It would be nice if we could stay on this island, but there isn't enough room for a campsite. We're going to have to cross to get to American Point. To say the least, it will be a difficult paddle. The secret is that you must keep your canoe heading directly into the wind or in an instant you'll get spun sideways. If that happens, you'll have to paddle with all your might to get the bow of the canoe pointed directly into the wind again. Whatever you do, don't quit! Give it all you've got, keep your wits about you, and we'll come out on the other side safely. Do you understand?"

The whole group looked at me with eyes as big as saucers. Several kids nodded their heads approvingly. Chris's face showed a resolve uncommon for someone so young. As we paddled just 100 yards out, a huge wind began to blow. I was in the lead canoe and had to set the pace. It was difficult as the waves would splash the person paddling in the front. Red was with me and we both were struggling. I kept looking back and noticed that Chris stayed in the rear, encouraging everyone else to keep going. He was not asked to do that but just sensed the need. Slowly but steadily, we were inching our way to American Point. Finally, our canoe was about 50 yards from the narrows leading to our campsite. We continued paddling and made it to the narrow opening. As we made it to the narrows, I looked back and saw the nearest canoe was about 100 yards behind but making steady progress.

"Oh my gosh Tom, this is really bad!" stated Red with a very concerned look on her face.

Above the crashing waves on the side of the canoe, the howling wind had picked up its pace. I hollered, "Don't quit! Keep on paddling." However, the other canoes were out too far to hear my voice.

"Tom, they're in trouble. Do you think they will all make it?" asked Red.

Chris was a strong paddler and was bringing up the rear.

"Keep going! We can make it!" I heard him holler confidently.

As we entered the narrows, the wind was shielded by the trees and the paddling became much easier.

Full of excitement, I yelled, "We made it, Red!"

Red and I beached and unloaded our canoe. The kids were still battling the wind and the waves. I dropped to my knees and prayed, asking God to keep all the kids safe. One by one they came in. I helped one of the students named Allison out of her canoe and she flopped into my arms sobbing. I held her in my arms and stroked her hair gently, trying to calm her down.

With tears streaming down her cheeks she whispered, "Mr. Hall, I didn't think we were going to make it. I thought I was going to die."

"Allison, I'm so proud of you! I saw a look of determination come over your face and you plowed right through that wind."

"Thanks for holding me. I'm alright now," Allison said in a strained but relieved voice.

The last canoe was Chris's. He staggered over to me and said, "Tom, that was as tough as it gets! Allison and Sandy were really struggling."

"Chris, thanks for hanging in there. They wouldn't have made it without you encouraging them the entire way. How are you doing?" I asked as I put my hand on his shoulder.

"I'm doing fine, Tom. My arms feel like rubber. I've never worked so hard in my life!"

"Everyone come close," I said loudly enough for everyone to hear, "This is our first campsite and we earned it. I'm so proud of all of you! It was probably the hardest paddle I've ever had."

In that moment, I shot up a prayer. Then I thought to myself, "What have I gotten myself into? "The responsibility was almost overwhelming.

"Hey Chris, let's go up this path and check out the latrine."

"Okay, Hallsey."

Chris followed me up the path.

"Chris, I was scared to death!"

"I know Tom, that was terrible. Is every day going to be like this one?"

"I sure hope not. How are you doing?" I asked Chris.

"I don't know. I'm still shaking. I really don't know how some of them made it. I just kept screaming, 'You got to keep going! Don't give up!' I honestly didn't think Allison and Sandy were going to make it, but they did it!"

It was a rough start to an incredible experience for all of us. Ranger Joe pulled up the next morning just after we had breakfast. Marian was all stitched up and glad to be back with the group.

I called the group together that morning once Marian was back with us. I explained to them that every morning, we would be having what I called a "Quiet Time." I informed them that we would set aside time every morning for each person to go off on their own within shouting distance of our camp and spend some time just soaking in the beauty that the BWCA afforded us. Quiet Time was a chance to enjoy the silence, maybe do some writing, or simply breathe in the fresh air and be still. I instructed them that there was to be no talking with others and that this was indeed a time where silence ruled. When I yelled the following chant, "Hi – why – enne – menne – key – key – ooo – cha – cha – anna – pee – wha – wha," the quiet time was over and the students were to return to the campsite and gather around the fire. Around the fire, anyone who wanted could share their personal experience during Quiet Time with the rest of the group. We grew as a family through this daily routine.

Every day, I looked forward to having Quiet Time. I would go off and write about the trip in the journals I brought with me. As I sat looking out into the quiet stillness of the majestic

natural surroundings of the BWCA, words just seemed to fly off my pen onto the paper. It was a relaxing exercise for me and enabled me to get my feelings down onto paper and process them as I wrote. My surroundings made me feel very small in the greater scheme of things, and I started to wonder how all this beauty came to be.

I knew one thing for sure. I LOVED the wilderness canoe camping experience. It was right up my alley! I loved every part of the experience from yanking a canoe right out of the water and portaging it overland to spending time in the bow, stern, or middle of the canoe as a duffer (I didn't do much of that) to cooking over an open fire. We would sing boisterously around a campfire and end up laughing like crazy. There was nothing like star gazing under a canopy of a million stars, watching a rainstorm roll in followed by a spectacular rainbow stretched from one end of the landscape to the other, or witnessing the Northern Lights dancing in the night sky. I saw wild bears in the camp and on the trail. I fished for walleye, lake trout, small and large mouth bass, and northern pike, all out of the most pristine water I have ever witnessed. I caught my first walleye up on Lake Saganaga in a small bay off one of the many little islands in that area. It was HUGE, and I have the photo to prove it. All of these Boundary Waters experiences were available to me in my home state of Minnesota.

I remember that walleye story a little differently. I thought you got that huge walleye in the bay just off the waterfalls by Jasper Lake. Anyway, it was a huge catch and you were so excited! That walleye provided a nice meal after I taught you how to clean it. It was some special memory!

This is how I remember it.

We went fishing at the base of some rapids. We figured fish would come in at dusk to find food washed in by the moving water. We were right! At first, Chris was fishing with a drop line from his canoe.

"What are you doing, Chris?" I inquired.

"This is the way my dad taught me to catch sunnies," Chris casually replied.

"We're not catching sunnies up here! Roll up that line and take my rod. Now cast it by that big rock. It has an orange Rapala on it."

"Okay, Hallsey."

He made a nice cast for a newbie and started reeling in the line. Then, WHAM! His rod bent sharply.

"Chris, you got a big one. Don't reel too fast. Just play the fish and tire him out."

Chris was so excited to have a fish on his line that it looked to me like he was in a different world. I wasn't sure if he was listening to me or not, but I kept coaching him on how to go about catching this apparently huge fish.

"Don't lose it. Keep the line tight and let the drag keep the line from breaking."

Finally, he brought it to the side of the canoe. Without a net in hand, I put both of my hands under the tired fish and literally scooped it up and into the canoe. It was a beautiful walleye.

"Wow! It's as big as a canoe paddle!" he exclaimed.

"Good job, Chris!" I affirmed him, just as excited as he was. The walleye was huge and a catch to be proud of!

We caught several walleyes. We put them on a stringer and brought them back to our camp. I showed Chris how to clean the fish and prepare them for cooking over a fire. Everyone was excited to have a meal of fresh fish for breakfast in the morning.

On a beautiful night in the Boundary Waters, Chris and I decided to go for an evening paddle. The two of us paddled down the middle of Jasper Lake. There was a slight breeze coming from the south. The water was completely still and looked like a plate of glass stretching before us into a full moon, its bright beam shining atop the water like a glass table.

"How about this evening, Chris? Can you believe there are problems in the world?"

"Hallsey, have you ever experienced a more perfect evening? I can't imagine anything better than this. I have the chills!"

The only sound was the paddles dipping into the water in perfect rhythm as the canoe skimmed over the lake. I took a deep breath and felt the pure oxygen flowing down my throat and into my lungs.

"Chris, I will cherish this moment forever!"

"Thank you, my friend, for making this experience the highlight of my life so far," Chris exclaimed.

We pulled into our campsite just as the fire was burning down to the coals. All the kids were in their tents sleeping.

"Put some wood on the fire," I requested as I went for my guitar.

Chris gathered some wood and placed it on the glowing embers. The fire began to blaze and grow, coming alive again.

"Let's stay up and talk and sing for a little while."

We began a comfortable conversation around the campfire. Chris told me about his family of three boys and four girls. We discovered that we were both the third child in big families. As the night went on, we got kind of crazy and began singing a little too loud.

"Have you ever heard the song 'Ghost Riders in the Sky?' "

"I don't think so," Chris answered.

"I can't remember all the words, but I'll sing a couple of lines while I play the guitar."

"An old cowpoke went riding out one dark and windy day,
Upon a ridge he rested as he went along his way
When all at once a mighty herd of red-eyed cows he saw
A-plowin' through the ragged sky and up a cloudy draw.
Yippie-yi-ooh, yippie-yi-yay, ghost riders in the sky."

We sang that song over and over again at the top of our lungs and broke into uncontrollable laughter. The kids began to stir and wonder what was happening to their leader. Finally, Chris and I slipped into our sleeping bags. As soon as we closed our eyes, we fell fast asleep.

On one of the days, when we were camped on Knife Lake, a rain storm came up very quickly. It got very dark and poured on us for about an hour. As quickly as it came upon us, the storm passed, leaving in its wake the most beautiful rainbow I had ever seen. It stretched from one end of the horizon to the other making a perfect arc. The colors were vibrant against the sunlit sky. Needless to say, this wasn't our last Boundary Waters trip together. There were a few more to come. However, a connection was made, a friendship began, and a wonderful story was about to emerge.

Later that same summer, my friend Jay Moore and I went to the BWCA in August to enjoy a week of canoe camping. I went as a co-counselor with Tom on another canoe trip with students in July of 1974.

Over Labor Day weekend in 1975, after graduating from high school, I returned to the BWCA with my buddy Gary Dahle. Being late in the season, we never saw the sun and it rained on us pretty much the whole time. I didn't mind it, but Gary hated it. When I recently asked him about the trip we took, he immediately recalled it and went on to explain how much he hated it because he was wet and miserable the whole time. That was a pretty good description of that trip.

My best friend from college, Mike Graber (I call him Grabes) and I took a canoe trip up into Canada's Quetico Region in 1977. We packed up my Green Lean, a 1967 Oldsmobile Delmonte 88 I bought for $300 cash, and headed north to the Gunflint Trail from Minneapolis. We canoed from Minnesota into the Quetico area and canoed the Wawiag River. On the Wawiag, we swamped the canoe I borrowed from Tom going down some rapids and put a hole in its side. We patched it up using pine tar and duct tape and continued on our route. We were so far into the wild that we didn't see any other people for days. One day, we decided to canoe in the nude when suddenly a small

plane came into view. The plane did a flyover and buzzed us a couple of times. I'm sure the pilot, whoever he or she was, enjoyed a good laugh. All we got was a sunburn...all over!

We went again in the summer of 1978 with Mike's buddy from Chicago and my brother David. It was a good trip, filled with a lot of laughter. We each acquired a nickname for various reasons. My brother David earned his nickname for stumbling over branches coming up out of the ground on portages. We called him "Trip Toe." Mike's friend earned the nickname "Hip Deep" because every time he went into the water, he would fall and get wet up to his hips. We called Grabes "Welt Head" because every time a mosquito or blackfly would bite him, a big welt would develop on the spot where he got bitten. I took us over a 120-rod portage and then realized it was the wrong portage. We had to trudge it all the way back to get back on track. That earned me the nick name "Wrong Way".

My last trip to the BWCA was with Grabes during the summer after we graduated from college in 1979. We shipped our gear up to Grand Marais via Greyhound and then tripped up there and back on a Honda 750 four motorcycle I bought that year from Mr. Grunke, my ninth-grade math teacher. We had a blast in the Boundary Waters once again.

The BWCA was the classroom in which I became one of Tom's students. Little did I know that this singular relationship would withstand the test of time and the trials that each of us would go through during our own valley and mountaintop experiences. Memories from past trips to the BWCA involve some of my very best of friends. My BWCA memories prevail over time and remind me of special moments with special people. Lord willing, I plan to return with Lisa and all our now young adult

children and their significant others for a special wilderness canoeing experience. Rain or shine, it will be an experience worth remembering.

No More Coach Hall

While Chris was in high school, he would stop by after school just to talk. He made the varsity high school hockey team as a sophomore, which was pretty incredible. He had a good year and enjoyed playing for my brother. I never saw Chris play, but I'm sure he had talent and I knew he loved the game!

I had follow-up visits to my cardiologist in December 1972, March 1973, and October 1973. During the October visit, I was told that I could not participate in high school varsity athletics due to the aortic insufficiency. Football was out, hockey was out of the question, but baseball was okay. This was devastating news to me. How the doctors made those determinations was beyond my body's comprehension. I could easily do everything they said I couldn't. I remember in that moment thinking to myself, "There is no way that I am going to just quietly go to the sidelines, or the end of the bench, and quit doing what I love to do." I determined then and there that I would keep doing every activity I could possibly do. I would monitor myself and then act depending on how my body felt and functioned.

Looking back on my determination to self-regulate, I can see how this decision has served me well over these past 47 years, keeping me functional and "in the game" if you will. My football days came to an end my sophomore year. I replaced playing football with more partying and pursuing relationships with girls. I was only able to connect with them on a surface level because of that lie I was believing that there was something wrong with me. I needed something more constructive to occupy myself and fill the void that was created when I wasn't allowed to participate in varsity sports.

During his junior year, Chris stopped by my classroom after school. He was obviously upset about something and wanted to talk.

"Hey, Chris! How are you doing?" I asked as I noticed a frown on his face. That was unusual because he was always smiling. I knew something was troubling him. "What's up?" I asked, trying to read his nonverbal communication.

"Your brother isn't coaching anymore."

"Yeah, he had trouble with some of the players last year," I commented.

"I know about that. We were playing up in Duluth when it happened. After the game, several players were drinking on the bus and the word got out about it. Your brother found out and wasn't too pleased to say the least."

"He felt the pressure of failing to control his team members on that trip. He talked to the principal and decided to step down from his coaching position. He had been coaching for many years and felt it was time for him to quit," I said.

"It wasn't his fault! I know those guys. No coach could control them! I was sorry to see him resign as our hockey coach."

"Who's the new coach?" I asked.

"A guy who coached the JV team," Chris replied.

"I know who he is. He knows hockey and should do a good job."

"I was looking forward to playing this year. We had to take a physical and they discovered a leaky valve in my heart, which I already knew about."

"So what happened?"

"I talked to the new coach. He didn't want to take responsibility for me playing with a heart condition. He said I could be skating hard on a lone break and have a heart attack. I tried to convince him that I can play. I already know about my leaky valve, but I've been playing hockey for many years and it's never bothered me. I begged him to let me play. He wasn't convinced, and said he wouldn't change his mind. He just didn't want the responsibility if something happened to me on the ice. He also said he was sorry because he knew I had speed and good talent. I'm sure your brother would've let me play. I hate the new guy!"

"Chris, you can't hate him. I understand where he's coming from. You have to forgive him."

"I can't, Hallsey! I love hockey and I want to play for Irondale with all my friends."

"It's not the end of the world, Chris."

"What would you have done if this happened to you? What if your coach told you that you couldn't play your junior year? Wasn't that the year that your team went to the state tournament?"

"I would have been devastated, Chris. I won't lie to you. At that time in my life, hockey meant everything to me. Now I understand why you're hurting so bad. I'm sorry this has happened to you. What are you going to do?"

"I don't know. Maybe I'll go to all the games and go up into the stands and pick fights."

"That won't help or solve anything."

"Yeah, I know, but I just can't stop playing hockey because some doctor says I can't and the coach is too scared to let me skate. I'm going to play somewhere!"

"What about your heart?"

"I can handle my heart!"

"Chris, this is a tough lesson for you. I hope you won't do something foolish. I have confidence in you and know that you will figure this out and do the right thing. I would've struggled too. Hockey was my life and it defined me! I feel your pain and I can empathize with how you're feeling when I place myself in your shoes. Please keep in touch and let me know how you're doing."

"Thanks for listening to me. I knew somehow that you would understand. I just had to get that off my chest. I don't know what I will do, but please don't worry because I'll be all right."

Chris left my classroom and I really felt bad for him. Right then and there I made a commitment to myself that I would pray for him daily.

I didn't go to many of the Irondale hockey games because it just hurt too much to watch all my friends play, knowing I could be out there skating as well if not for the new coach and the decision he made to treat me like an invalid.

Someone told me about the Lake Region midget hockey team soon after I left the ice at Irondale for the last time. I didn't need a physical to join. I walked into a locker room for the first practice and Coach Wilson threw the captain's band at me and announced in front of the whole team, "You're our captain!" I was surprised no one said anything about it.

I ended up playing more hockey games than my high school team did...all with a "bad" heart.

I played baseball my junior year and was a captain for the team my senior year. I lettered in both soccer and baseball my senior year. Unexpectedly, the soccer coach approached me one day towards the end of my junior year and asked if I might consider playing soccer as a goalkeeper. I had never entertained the idea until then. I went to my cardiologist and pretty much convinced him that all I had to do was stand in the goal. He reluctantly gave me permission and unknowingly launched me into the game of soccer, which I played through college along with baseball and hockey. In college, I didn't need a physical to play.

Tom and I love the game of hockey. We both loved to play and grew up playing at the Minneapolis park board rinks and then skated on into high school and college. It was a common bond that we shared, along with all the ups and downs that came with it in both of our lives.

Chris stopped by a couple of weeks later and told me he was playing midgets. This was a club team that played a tough schedule. Hockey would still be a huge part of his life.

Unlike my teenage self, Chris liked a lot of girls and had some girlfriends in high school. But there was one girl he especially cared for. She was the daughter of one of my co-workers at Pike Lake. She went on one of the canoe trips to the BWCA after her younger sister participated one summer. She was in John Jones's group, so I never really got to know her. But if she was anything like her mom, she was a very special gal. Chris and I talked about her from time to time. He really cared for her, but her affections were for another guy. I mostly listened as he explained how he felt about her. I didn't know her so I couldn't give much advice. I just told him to respect her and treat her like a lady. He agreed.

Yeah, okay, back to hockey. My midget team turned out to be a great experience with a fun group of guys. We won our division, beating Minnetonka to go on to the state playoffs. We took third place in the state tournament up in International Falls. The next year, I ended up playing on a Junior B squad that had some of the same players on it that I had played with before during my sophomore year at Irondale. I kept skating and playing hockey into my sophomore year in college.

Irondale High School

After attending Marshall High School for seventh grade, our family of seven started to grow out of our house on the corner of 13th and Talmage. My parents decided to move into a newly built home. The home happened to be in New Brighton and was about three blocks away from where my childhood friend Jay lived on the Bright Wood Hills Golf Course. Our relationship began again, almost as if it had never been interrupted.

That's amazing that your parents would buy a house so close to your childhood friend so you and Jay could easily continue your friendship. A divine appointment, maybe!

In eighth grade I met Gary Dahle. His dad owned the golf course in New Brighton. Jay, Gary and I became best friends as we entered our teen years. We were pretty much inseparable. We attended High View Junior High where we played football, hockey and baseball. We also started partying during our junior high days. It's pretty incriminating just reading through my junior high and high school yearbooks. Lots of references to drinking, partying, and names of girls. I liked a lot of girls, but there were only a select few that I really liked...a lot!

That's one way we're not alike...I was pretty much the opposite of a ladies' man.

There was one girl I especially liked. I had my eye on her through eighth and ninth grade and finally got together with her in tenth grade. Her name was Leslie. Our relationship was off and on through our high school years. The trouble was that Jay was attracted to her as well and ended up dating her after I somehow broke up with her. It really bugged me because I still liked her a lot. One night, we were out carousing around the neighborhood, which had expanded in its breath and width, and somehow Jay and I got into a scrape over this. It was totally my doing as Jay was not the fighting type. I ended up punching my best friend in the face...over a girl...a girl who ended up with someone other than either of us! I felt awful and later apologized. Jay gracefully accepted my apology and we never talked about it again.

Jay, Gary and I went through our sophomore, junior, and senior years at Irondale High School. I experienced some devastating news in tenth grade when I found out about my bad valve, which kept me out of playing high school hockey and football my junior and senior years.

In baseball, I played center field. I enjoyed seeing the whole field of play. With my speed, I often caught balls for outs that normally would have dropped in for hits. I remember a playoff game for baseball during my senior year. Leslie happened to come watch the game. If we won the game, we went to the playoffs. If we lost, our season was over. The game came down to the last inning. We were up by one run and needed one more out to win the game. The opposing team had runners on second

and third. The guy at bat lined a shot straight at me out in center field. I mistakenly came in on the ball to make the catch but misjudged how hard the ball had been hit, which I realized too late. I stopped, frantically ran back to make the catch, and missed the ball. The ball rolled out to the fence, allowing the runs to score and ending our season. I was embarrassed and felt so bad for letting down my team that I just sat down in center field and watched the other team celebrate. Knowing that Leslie witnessed my error made it all the more painful.

I played center field in baseball too! Defensively, I was a good outfielder and had a strong arm. One time, I ran for a catch and it dropped in front of me. I threw the ball in and was walking back to my position, when I heard a crack. I looked up and saw the ball sailing over my head. The pitcher didn't wait for me to get back to my position, apparently. Because of that, we lost a close game…and it was my fault. That's always the worst feeling!

As juniors, Leslie and I somehow ended up emceeing Irondale's Ice Age Coronation program. I can't remember if we were going out with each other or not at the time. She looked beautiful and did a great job, kissing every guy she crowned in each class. I, on the other hand, caused her to shed some tears when I mistakenly crowned the wrong queen! After crowning the gal whose name I thought corresponded with the name of the winner, Leslie came to me with tears in her eyes and whispered into my ear, "Chris, you crowned the wrong person."

I was beside myself! I immediately went back out onto the stage, admitted my error, and apologetically took the crown

from the gal I mistakenly crowned and gave it to the gal whose name did correspond with the name of the winner. Oops! Sorry, Georgene. Sorry, Julie. Sorry, Leslie. At least now all three of you have a good story to share. I took some flack for my mishap, which became obvious when friends wrote in my yearbook about my blunder. It was a humbling experience to say the least. For the rest of the year, it seemed like either Georgene or Julie just happened to be around every corner as I went from class to class through the day. I must have apologized to both a thousand times.

Jay continued playing hockey and started to play golf instead of football, doing very well at it. Jay won the Elvis Presley look-alike contest at school two years in a row. I remember seeing him do his impersonation of Elvis to the delight of every girl in the crowd. I was struck by his stage presence at the time because neither of us ever did anything having to do with acting or singing. His dance moves were Elvis all the way and he looked exactly like him onstage!

As Jay entered his senior year, he put on a few extra pounds and the nickname "Morsels" was placed upon him by someone…I'm not sure who. I remember watching him at a hockey game and noticing that he fell a lot on the ice. At the time, I remember thinking that was a little weird. I knew Jay could skate a lot better than he was. I figured it was due to the extra weight he was carrying. I also noticed something was a bit off when we were partying. As we drank and partied, it seemed like Jay was always way over the edge, more so than the rest of us who hung out together. He would often lose his balance while getting in and out of his car. I just figured he was partying a little heavier than the rest of us. Yet I had this strange feeling that something about Jay wasn't right. We graduated from high school together, which for me just didn't feel like a big deal. I was off to college, but it was the beginning of a fatal year for Jay.

Sharing Life's Experiences

Chris graduated from high school in 1975. He decided to go to college in Rockford, Illinois. We saw each other during the summer. Chris told me that he was accepted into college and asked if we could write each other during the school year. I agreed and told him that if he would write me, I would answer his letters. I gave him my address. He did write, but I didn't always answer his letters.

I went away to Rockford College in Rockford, Illinois on a soccer scholarship as a goalkeeper, one of the saving graces for me in high school when the heart valve kept me out of football and hockey. I played soccer for two years in high school, which led to me being recruited as a keeper for Rockford College.

One time I wrote and said, "Chris, I owe you three letters." He wrote back and said, "Tom, you owe me nothing." He freed me up with that statement! I realized Chis wanted to stay in touch. As a result, I was more faithful in answering his letters. This is a response letter that I sent to Chris during the fall of 1975.

Dear Chris,

Thanks for your letter. I really enjoyed hearing from you. I want you to know that I consider you a very personable and warm friend. I'm answering your letter right away because if I don't, I'll let it slide and you won't ever hear from me.

It sounds like you're jumping into college life pretty heavy. That's good, but be careful to allow enough time for your studies. Don't be afraid to say no to some of those commitments.

Things are going smoothly back here. I'm into my job again, no real problems or hassles with any of my students. I'm busy with my house. Seems like I have a lot of projects going. I'm putting on a new roof and making a bedroom in my basement for Mike. The only problem is I'm not spending enough time with my wife and kids. That's one of the things that frustrates me a bit because I don't like to spend time with them when I feel obligated or out of a sense of duty, but I really love to be with them and enjoy their company. I'm not expressing myself very well, but I think you know what I mean.

I spent three days up at Jasper Falls a couple of weeks ago with some friends. We never saw the sun once. It was cold and wet. We caught only one fish, but still had a good time. Can you believe that? I love the wilderness and the Boundary Waters keeps calling me back there.

I think I'll be giving up hockey this year and spending time skating in my backyard with my kids. I flooded the rink for them in my back yard. If you're home on break, maybe you can come over and skate with us sometime.

Well, Chris, I think I'll close now. So take care and hang in there!

Love,
Tom

P.S. I talk with Leslie's mom from time to time. She's a paraprofessional at my school. I think Leslie likes you a lot. I think you're better off playing it cool and not coming on too strong. Play it your own way, okay?

Chris saved all the letters that I sent to him. Somehow, we both felt it was important to stay in touch during his college experience. I continued to pray for him and secretly hoped that someday he would surrender his heart to Jesus Christ, the same one I surrendered my heart to when I was just a young boy.

It was at college that I heard about Jay being sick. We had exchanged a letter or two after I left Minneapolis for Rockford. He enrolled at Anoka Ramsey Technical School and started taking some classes, ceramics was one of them. According to his letter, Jay was playing a lot of pool for free at the college. When I visited him during Thanksgiving, he was not himself, which caused me concern. As I returned to college, I remember turning towards God and asking God to heal Jay and feeling like that was exactly what God was going to do. This was probably the first time I ever really thought seriously about God being someone you could pray to, let alone someone who listened to those prayers.

Later, after returning to college, I received word that Jay wasn't doing very well. I received a mixture of letters from a few different people about Jay's condition. Some of those letters relieved my concerns and a few of them painted a very grim outlook. Later that same year, I received the news that Jay had died of a brain tumor.

This all happened during Chris's freshman year. He was devastated.

I hitchhiked home for Jay's funeral. Somber and silently, I made my way home with a trucker who brought me into Minneapolis from Wisconsin someplace.

Chris came home for the funeral and needed to talk to someone. He contacted me and we got together over a cup of coffee.

"Tom, I just lost my best friend! We did everything together. We've known each other for a long time. We grew up together, played sports together, and hung out whenever we could. When I left for college, he had something wrong with his brain. I didn't think it was serious and was sure he would get over it. Then I heard he had died and I just had to come home. I knew his family well. I saw his parents and they were crushed. They knew we were close friends and tried to comfort me. Can you imagine...they lost their son, and they were trying to comfort me? It broke my heart to talk to them."

I just listened as Chris told stories about what he and Jay did during their short time together on earth.

"Chris, I've never lost a friend. I know you are struggling over the loss," I responded.

I wanted to share the gospel with Chris, but knew it just wasn't the right time. He was really hurting and needed to talk and share his feelings. Jay seemed like a great friend and someone Chris would miss dearly. There was nothing that I could say that would comfort him. So, I just listened.

At Jay's wake, I cried my heart out kneeling by the coffin in which his lifeless body was placed. I served as a pallbearer at

his funeral at St. John's Catholic Church. I noted the spot in the cemetery in St. Anthony where they buried Jay's body and have often returned to it through the years to give my regards.

In my grief, I wrote the following poem.

Why?
My friend just died. I cried.
Looking to the heavens, to the sky,
I asked the question, "Why?"
No reply.

I'm packing a bag, I'm returning home.
Now sitting on the side of the road, tears aflow,
Still asking the question, "Why?"
Still no reply.

This is my friend, my very good friend.
Now at his funeral, sobbing at his side,
Why, why, why?
No reply.

I could see it in his eyes, I could feel it in my bones.
My friend's demise, ever so slow, till death swallowed whole,
Why?
Please, please…reply.
Give me an answer for my "why."

Down deep in my gut, there existed a feeling that I was responsible for that tumor that developed in Jay's brain. That punch I threw when we were 16 landed hard on Jay's head. With

that plate still in his head, it may have caused something to take place that otherwise might not have had to happen. It's a thought that nags me to this day, even so many years later. I may never know, but I do know this...Jay's passing somehow brought me closer to believing in God, even though God did not answer my prayers to heal Jay.

At the time, I was not a believer in anything but myself. I was brought up in the Catholic religion, but didn't really know anything about God that I could be sure about. But my first encounter with the death of my very good friend drew me closer to God, whoever or whatever this mysterious "God" was. Jay's death caused me to feel the frailness of life and the brevity with which we exist on this earth, in this world, amongst and with each other.

I did what most people do after losing someone they love, whether that's a spouse, a child, or a friend. I just determined to keep living and doing what I was doing. I threw myself into studies, sports, carousing, and partying...not necessarily in that order.

A few months later, it was my time to suffer. My brother Dave was struggling with a cancer tumor behind his rib cage. They did exploratory surgery and could not remove the tumor. Dave died December 7,1976 at age 42. I was crushed. I prayed with all the faith I had that God would heal him and when God didn't, I was devastated.

I shared my broken heart with Chris in this letter I wrote to him while he was at college.

Dear Chris,

This letter comes to you with a heavy heart and much sadness. My brother Dave died Tuesday, December 7 at 9:30 PM. He was so weak. It was a blessing the illness didn't linger.

You knew Dave. He was your coach and teacher. Maybe you can share my sadness as I grieve his loss. The grief that fills my life, however, is not for Dave but for me. Dave is no longer suffering but at peace with Jesus and loved ones in heaven. Someday I will be with Dave and spend eternity with him and never be separated again! But my heaviness is because I must continue and walk the course that he set.

My brother Bob gave the eulogy at the memorial service. Bob showed a lot of inner strength and courage as he spoke of my brother's life in our family. He told of such things as Dave being a substitute father and a real inspiration and example to us boys and our sister. He told of how he took part in and included us in many of his activities. He bought us skates and hockey sticks and coached each of us. He provided us with leadership and felt responsible as the firstborn to keep our family together. He had us saving our pennies, nickels, and dimes because he had a dream to buy lake property. He spoke to us boys after sibling rivalry had run its course. We bought some lakeshore property in Wisconsin. We cleared the land. Brick by brick we built a boathouse and our cabin together. We learned we had so much in common and learned to love each other. But Bob said that Dave would not want us to honor and glorify him this day, but rather God, whom Dave had learned to love so much. Dave had two events which changed the course of his walk. One was the death of our dad and the other was the death of his young son, Danny, whom he greatly loved. Danny's death also greatly impacted his wife, Marilyn. Dave, a person who could have become cynical and bitter, became warm, loving, and giving, which was his greatest quality. He gave freely of his means, his time, and himself to others, to whom he reached out and touched in so many wonderful ways. There was quite a definite move in his life from the physical and material, to a life of spiritual growth. He was a good son, brother, father, and friend. I'm sure God welcomed him into heaven with open arms!

> I grieve and my heart is heavy at the loss of my brother. I loved him so much and part of him lives inside of my body. I will continue on the course that he set. God in time will heal my hurt.
>
> With much love,
> Tom

I remember receiving this letter from Tom about Dave. I wanted to return home and attend Dave's funeral, but I was in the middle of finals and couldn't get away from school. I didn't fully comprehend Tom's letter. I'm sure the spiritual aspect of it went right by me, but the part about Dave's character I could wholeheartedly relate to after having Dave as a teacher and a coach. I heard that many of the guys I played varsity hockey with attended Dave's funeral. What a sign of respect for a man who sacrificed much for those he taught and coached.

In college over my entire four-year experience, I was an average student with a 2.68 cumulative grade point. My grade points through the semesters ranged from a low of 2.29 to a high of 3.50. I roomed with four different guys in three different types of accommodations while at Rockford. My freshman roommate was a big guy named John Boyd. His favorite outfits were always overalls. Despite our differences, we hit it off and became good friends. I got to know his family who lived in Rockford, and we often went to John's house for a good meal or something to eat after we had been out drinking. John and his sister both had jumpers, horses that were trained to jump over things. I was invited to ride a couple times and really enjoyed

it. The feeling of jumping a horse is like none other: Each jump is very rhythmic and fluid, requiring good balance and timing. Through a variety of experiences, John and his family became very dear to me and we remain good friends to this day.

I was a resident assistant during my junior year and enjoyed a single room that had a private bath and shower. Mike Graber and I met through soccer. We became very good friends and roomed together during our sophomore and senior years. Mike had an infectious laugh that cracked me up, and we enjoyed some very good times together on and off campus. He remains my closest college friend and lives in Valparaiso, Indiana.

During the spring of my sophomore year, Tom invited me to be a counselor at an environmental camp with him and his students for a few days. It turned out to be a very positive and rewarding experience as I engaged with elementary age students. The kids really accepted me, and I seemed to be able to relate to them very well. Because of this experience, I switched my major from Science to Child Development with the intent to be a classroom teacher in elementary education rather than teach science at the high school level. This proved to be a great move and my student teaching experience confirmed it. I loved working with elementary age students between third and sixth grade. I wasn't all that keen on lesson plans as Mrs. Porter, my supervising teacher, would often remind me, but she liked the way I mixed it up with the students. Mrs. Porter saw the teacher in me and encouraged me to pursue teaching as a career.

I did well in all my classes related to education. In everything else school was a bit of a struggle, although I really enjoyed my creative writing, zoology, and history classes.

Rockford is a liberal arts college, so I was exposed to a very well-rounded course of studies that ranged from Adult Orientation to Physical Education to Introduction to Economics. The varied coursework included Elements of Statistics, Genetics and Chemistry, Fundamentals of Music, Introduction to Cultural Anthropology...and the list goes on. The only class I dropped out of was chemistry. After just a few days of Dr. Crawford's chemistry class, I was swimming in the deep end without an end in sight. I think I replaced it with an economics class on investments. My lowest grade was a "D" that my Fundamentals of Music teacher rewarded me with. I'm sure he wanted to fail me. I had to sing the scale solo for him. He was not very encouraging in the face of my severe stage fright at the time. He could not understand why I was unable to do such a simple thing. For the life of me, I couldn't either.

My studies in college were eclipsed by all the partying that started during the first few days of orientation. I got some strange looks from the Dean of Student Services when I carried all my belongings into my dorm suite, which I was sharing with three other guys. I packed all my stuff into empty Pabst Blue Ribbon beer cases, so it looked like all that I was carrying into my dorm was cases of beer. I guess the shoulder length hair, boots, and jeans didn't help much either. After getting settled in, the partying started. Drinking, smoking pot, and women, women, women. The only thing that broke that cycle was sleeping, eating, and sports. This continued through all four years of college, a never-ending cycle that took its toll on me physically and emotionally.

I attended Rockford on a soccer scholarship as a goalkeeper, but I also played baseball for Rockford and hockey for Rock Valley Junior College.

Rockford's soccer program was mediocre, but it gradually increased in depth and breadth over the four years I was there. I started out in the goal not knowing much, but playing a lot. I picked up the nickname "Rock" when a friend of mine on the team was looking over my shoulder reading a letter I received from my buddy Gary Dahle. Gary had started his letter to me with the words, "Hey Rockfish." My friend from Missouri laughed and blurted out, "Rockfish!"

I looked at him and very seriously said, "Don't even think about it." He looked at me, smiled and said,

"Okay, then...Rock. Yeah...Rock." That nickname stuck with me all though college.

My salvation in soccer came when I attended a goalkeepers' camp in Connecticut. It helped me sharpen the skills a keeper needs and helped me understand the position much more. I returned to Rockford directly from the camp and went right into my first soccer practice noticeably a different keeper. We enjoyed a Cinderella season my junior year, and I racked up some shut-out minutes that might still be a record today.

Rock Valley Junior College had a club hockey team and offered a swimming class at Rockford College because the junior college didn't have a pool. I registered for the swimming class, which made me eligible to play on the hockey team. I never attended the swimming class, but somehow I was able to keep playing hockey for Rock Valley. The first year was a blast getting to know a new group of guys, and we did all sorts of crazy things on and off the ice. The second year was not as much

fun. The coach brought some goons onto the team to serve as enforcers. Every time one of these guys got touched, he would drop his gloves and fight. The fans didn't like it, I hated it, and it only served to pull our team down. I played the rest of the season, but then the next year I was faced with the decision of playing with a Junior A team and traveling a lot or hanging it up to focus on getting a college education. I decided to focus on my education.

I enjoyed playing baseball while in college. I kept to centerfield where I made some nice catches on the fly and stole a lot of bases. About this time, my eyesight started to change, which affected my hitting and the way I ran down a ball in the outfield. My senior year was a bit of a wash, because I suffered from an ailment that involved my pointer and middle fingers on both of my hands. I couldn't play for most of the season because of this condition, which persisted almost into May. I tried to play towards the end of the season, but I had lost some weight and lots of strength. When I did return to play, I was easily thrown out trying to steal second base in one of the last games of the season. I thought that was the end of my baseball days, but I returned 22 years later to play for a 35 and over team called the Minnetonka Mustangs in the Federal League in Minnesota. I'm still playing on this team at the age of 62. I recently played in Rockford's 2019 alumni baseball game and was by far the oldest guy on the field. Still living the dream as they say!

Chris and I wrote to each other during the four years he was in college. We came together during the summer and went out for coffee from time to time. Toward the end of his senior year, he asked me to attend his college graduation. I checked with Sandy and she gave me the "okay." When the time came, I rode down to the Rockford area with Chris's parents and younger siblings.

I carefully considered what I could give Chris as a graduation present. I decided to write him a letter and give him a Bible. I can't remember exactly all the things I said in that letter. Among other things, I know that I said I appreciated our friendship, but it had plateaued and couldn't go any deeper. I told him there was a side of me that he knew nothing about. I bought him a Bible. I wrote him a personal letter that I placed inside the front of the Bible. On the front inside cover, I wrote him a little note and referenced a verse from the last book in the Bible called Revelation.

I wrapped the Bible with the letter inside and planned to give it to him just as we were leaving. My plan was to not have him open it until we left. I didn't know how he would respond to receiving a Bible. For all I knew, he might have thrown it at me if he wasn't interested.

It was a small college and the students all seemed to know each other. His graduation was a joyous occasion, and I was impressed with the music and speeches. His family and I had breakfast together with Chris the next morning. After breakfast, we loaded up in Chris's parents' car. Just before leaving for the trip back home, I handed Chris my wrapped graduation gift and asked him to open it after we left. Chris was graduating with a teaching degree and would be seeking a job back in Minneapolis.

The Day After Graduating

I graduated from college on May 20, 1979 from Rockford College (now Rockford University) in Rockford, Illinois. I invited Tom to my college graduation. He agreed to come and drove with my parents, Ed and Grace, to Rockford from Minneapolis with the youngest siblings in my family: Ellen, David and Britta. Tom attended my college graduation ceremony with my family members. Afterwards, Tom and I went for a walk along a path through a wooded area that ran alongside the property line of the college. During that walk, we talked about many things. Towards the end of our walk I stopped, turned towards Tom, and asked, "Tom, do you know anything about a personal relationship with Jesus Christ?"

He responded by saying, "Yeah, a little."

That's all he said, and we completed the rest of our stroll through the woods without saying anything about it.

For the life of me, I have no idea where that question came from. Months before my graduation from college, I mysteriously developed ulcers on the tips of my index and middle fingers on both of my hands. Each of the sores had a little crusted-over circle in the middle that seemed to be connected to a nerve underneath. The two at the end of my middle fingers were more painful than the two on the ends of my index fingers. If I would bump the ends of these open sores, pain would shoot all the way up my arms into my armpits and just hang there until the pain subsided. I began standing with my fingers tucked under my armpits to protect them from bumping into anything and to keep them warm, which helped them feel a little better.

This condition lasted several months and kept me from playing a full season of baseball my senior year. I went to the nearby clinic and saw a doctor about the condition. The doctor told me never to reach into the refrigerator without wearing gloves and gave me some ointment to put on the open sores. That was a wasted trip to the clinic.

The pain would throb when I laid down to go to bed at night, so I spent a good deal of time trying to catch some sleep sitting upright in an armchair. I lost about 15 pounds, which for my already-lean body type made me look ghostly and pale. I wasn't sleeping, I wasn't eating, and I was getting behind in my studies.

I had a friend type up a final paper for one of my education classes because I literally could not do it. My friend volunteered to do it for me, but totally messed up the paper by filling it with spelling errors and omitting some of the content I had in the original draft. It was the only grade below an A I received on my courses having to do with my Child Development major. I reluctantly handed it in with a note to my professor about what happened and why. My professor didn't consider the circumstances and marked me down.

Finally, without any answers from the medical community, I got so frustrated that I sat down in the armchair in our dorm room with determination. I strategically placed my thumbnail and the nail of my fourth finger under the crusted circle on the opposite hand and yanked the tip of it off. This proved to be excruciatingly painful every time I did it to each of my fingers, but in time the sores healed over. Eventually I was on the mend with no more pain, but very calloused finger tips.

During this time, when I was feeling very down and tired, I happened to sit down in front of the television to take a break and watch what I thought was the beginning of a war flick of some kind. As I watched, the war images subsided and Reverend Billy Graham appeared on the screen and began talking. As I listened, I was surprised to find that tears started rolling down my face. I had no idea why I was crying. I think this is where the question I asked Tom about a personal relationship with Jesus Christ came from. I got up from the television, turned it off, and walked outside.

Outside, a light snow had fallen, which was a strange occurrence in the month of April in Illinois. I recall walking out the door of my dorm, heading out towards Fisher Chapel, and seeing my footprints in the snow behind me as I walked. The chapel was a place I had gone into only once before. There, I shook my fist at God after receiving news of my friend Jay's death. This was the only time I went to the chapel during my college years. Now, I found myself at the back side of the chapel and tried the door, which was locked. I went around to the other side of the chapel and almost kept walking, but something outside of me turned me around and led me up the short pathway to the other door. Upon pulling on it, I discovered it was open. Someone had locked the door, but the closed latch was laying against the outside of the door frame, causing the door to remain slightly ajar.

I went in and sat down. No one else was nearby or anywhere in the building. I'm not sure for how long I sat, but I recall the feelings and emotions that were running through me. I wasn't shaking my fist at God like I did last time. Instead I was tired, underweight, and worn down thinking about my life and especially my last four years attending Rockford.

Just before the condition with my fingers, I was becoming very uneasy about the things I was doing and had always been doing. Yes, I graduated from high school and was about to graduate from college. But through all these years I was drinking, chasing women, and smoking marijuana. There were some relationships with women that left me feeling guilty and empty, causing me to be very contemplative about my life. A couple relationships I had were just outright wrong. One in particular really caused me some serious consternation about my own behavior. My philosophy on life was, "Try anything once and if you don't like it, don't do it again." The problem with that philosophy is that you can try something once and it might just kill you! Any of my accomplishments educationally or in sports didn't really fill the void I was feeling in my life. It was the same old stuff and wasn't making me happy, content or fulfilled at all. As I sat and considered my past and my future, my thoughts drifted away from any conclusions, and I left the chapel as emptied as I was when I entered.

Chris, as you went through this struggle and headed toward the chapel, I can't help but think that the Holy Spirit was working in your life. My prayers were being answered and God was dealing with you. You were hearing His voice, but not identifying it or realizing quite what to do. This was the early stages of your spiritual journey before you surrendered your life to Jesus Christ.

I think you are probably right, Tom. I think God has always been there, desiring for me to know Him. But I just wanted to do things my way, until the things I was doing my way proved to be unfulfilling, vain, and short-lived. I was searching for something more than me and didn't know where to look.

The morning after I graduated from Rockford College, my parents, family members, and Tom met me at a restaurant called Stash O'Neils just off campus on State Street, where I bartended as I attended Rockford. We enjoyed a meal together before they all departed for Minnesota. Outside the restaurant, Tom handed me a wrapped gift and asked me not to open it until after he left with my family. I smiled, looked at him with some curiosity, and agreed. As soon as they all left, I tore into the gift Tom had given me.

I knew it was some sort of book. To my surprise, it was a new black Bible. I didn't own a Bible. We never had one in our home. I had never read anything directly from a Bible. When Jay and I went canoe camping off the Gunflint Trail, we stayed at a hotel the night before returning home. There was a Gideon's Bible in our room. I took it from the room when we left Grand Marais and gave it to Leslie as a joke when I got back to New Brighton. I was amused and curious. At this point in my life I had known Tom and his family for six years. They had often prayed at their dinner table when they invited

me to eat with them. Tom had never overtly talked to me about God or the Bible or church.

Inside the Bible was a note written on the inside of the front cover and an envelope containing a letter Tom wrote to me. This Bible and the contents I mentioned above was misplaced during a fundraising event for EPPIC Ministries in 1996 at Hope Presbyterian Church. What I remember from the note Tom wrote on the inside front cover was this:

> Dear Chris,
>
> Congratulations on graduating from college. You've worked hard and are ready for entering into your career as a teacher. You'll make a great teacher and influence the lives of many of your students. This book has become my very "best friend." It is my source of strength and encouragement. It is my hope that you find all that you need for life and living within its pages. My verse for you is found in Revelations 3:20. May God bless you in the days to come and all that follows.
>
> Your friend,
> Tom

I wasn't much of a writer back then, but God was using my limited writing ability to get to you. Evidently, I didn't feel right about talking with you openly about Jesus Christ.

Writing is very effective because you can read it over and over again. Also, you couldn't really debate or question what I was trying to say to you in the form of a letter. God was opening the door to your heart for you to have a relationship with Him and a deeper relationship with me. I knew in my heart it was only a matter of time!

Since God is perfect, it only follows that His timing is perfect.

The letter Tom wrote was enclosed in a white envelope and placed in the front cover of the Bible. He summarized my high school experience in a way that both surprised me and endeared him more to me than I thought possible. He knew me...but he didn't...he didn't know the real me. Very eloquently, he described the crush I felt losing Jay and the frustration I felt when my love for a certain girl didn't pan out. He encouraged me through words that described qualities in me I didn't see in myself. It was a letter I needed to receive in the face of the burdens I was carrying with respect to my own behavior over the past eight years going through high school and college.

After finishing the letter, I turned my attention to Revelation 3:20. I figured it was in the table of contents, so I looked for the word Revelation and found that there were contents for what was called the Old Testament and the New Testament. Under the New Testament contents, I found the word Revelation at the end of all the other names with the page number 1130 to the side of the word. I turned to that page and found Revelation at the top of the page. Then I realized it was divided into chapters with each sentence in each chapter numbered. With this realization, I turned to the third chapter and easily found the number 20. That specific sentence, was highlighted with

a yellow marker. I figured Tom must have done that. I read these words:

> *"Here I am! I stand at the door and knock.*
> *If anyone hears my voice and opens the door,*
> *I will come in and eat with that person, and*
> *they with me." (Revelation 3:20)*

These words cut quick to my heart and unknowingly began my spiritual journey and pursuit of knowing Jesus Christ and making Him known.

After reading the verse, I began to weep. Something inside of me just broke. Tears flowed from someplace deep within my soul. The words were speaking directly to my heart. It was as if God Himself was speaking directly to me in my circumstance and situation. God was wrapped up in my emotions and intellect and speaking words to me that were perfectly clear, meeting me right where I was at in my tiredness and brokenness.

I knew I needed to do a 180-degree about-face and start walking towards God. I wanted that relationship. I was hearing His voice. I wanted to open the door, but I didn't know how to do that. I returned to my dorm room and didn't speak to anyone about this.

I planned to visit Tom once I returned home to Minnesota. I wanted him to really know me and felt the need to tell him about all the stuff I was into so that we wouldn't have anything between us going forward. I was carrying a load of guilt I didn't know what to do with. It felt like I had a grand piano on my back that was weighing heavily upon me and pulling me down. All through my senior year, I felt like I was being consumed by something outside of myself. Something depressive! Something evil! The things I had been doing were not fulfilling, and my conscience was convicting me of the error of my ways. Amazingly, God used one verse read directly from the Bible to pick me up and turn me around, setting me on a course of learning I neither desired, sought, or knew I needed.

Tom has always been at the forefront of my spiritual journey which started when he met me and began praying that I would come to know Jesus. For six years before giving me the Bible, he purposed to pray for me every day and has kept it up throughout our relationship. I was totally unaware that he was doing this for me. Tom's practice has extended to praying for my children by name and for my ministry. The letter Tom wrote to me and placed in an envelope inside the Bible was written with more compassion, understanding, and love that I had ever experienced to that day. Tom wrote to me with such intimacy as only a good friend can do, which only served to endear him to me more.

A New Beginning: May 26th, 1979

After returning home from graduating from college, I went to Tom's house, determined to tell him about all the rotten stuff I had done and was doing. I thought for sure he wouldn't want anything to do with me after my confession. I had written and told Tom about what had happened after he left Rockford's campus: the experience I had in the open field as I read his letter, the note inside the front cover of the Bible, and the verse from Revelation. I had questions and lots of them.

I was sitting peacefully in my home one evening when I heard a knock on my front door. I opened the door and to my amazement, there stood Chris unannounced. "Chris, what's up?" I asked with a surprised expression on my face. "Come on in." He entered my home and we headed for my screened-in porch. It was a cool May evening.

"Do you want a cup of coffee?" I offered.

"No, I'm fine," he stated as he sat in an empty chair on the porch. I sat on the one beside him and we began to talk.

"How does it feel to be a college graduate?"

"It feels good! Now I have to find some employment."

"What are you looking for?"

"I want a teaching position. Preferably fourth or fifth grade."

"Hey, thanks for inviting me to your college graduation ceremony. I enjoyed meeting your college buddies. It was great being with your family as you went through the ceremony. It was way different than my graduation from the University of Minnesota. Mine was very impersonal and yours was warm and intimate."

"Thanks for the Bible and the letter you wrote me. I appreciated the letter and was amazed at how well you know me," said Chris, looking deep into my eyes.

Wow! I thought to myself. *Maybe this will be the conversation that I've waited for all these years!* I sat pondering that thought in my heart.

"I'm not the person you think I am!" Chris exclaimed. "I've done some terrible things that I'm not proud of. The guilt I feel related to these things is weighing on me, and I don't know what to do about it."

I knew I just needed to listen to him. Chris shared with me things that he had done in high school and college that he was not proud of. Some of them were pretty bad!

Finally, I interjected.

"Chris, you don't need to tell me all these things."

"Yes, I do! I want you to know the other side of me, the side you've never seen."

"Chris, can I show you some things that are in the Bible that relate to how you're feeling?" I asked.

"Sure," he responded enthusiastically. I grabbed my Bible that was sitting on the coffee table next to my chair.

"Look at Romans chapter 3, verse 23," I said as I handed Chris the Bible and showed him where the verse was in the New Testament. He read the verse silently to himself and then remarked,

"It says here that all have sinned and fall short of the glory of God. I know I fall short, but I don't see you as a sinner, Tom!"

"I sin every day by being selfish, disrespectful, prideful, and disobedient! The things you've done are no different than these. Right here in Romans it says that all have sinned and fall short of the glory of God. That includes both of us. As a matter of fact, that includes everyone."

"Wow, Tom, that's hard to believe."

"The Bible also says that the wages of sin is death, but the gift of God is eternal life through Jesus Christ our Lord," I quoted from memory. "That's found in Romans 6:23. Look here," I said as I turned the pages in the Bible to the sixth chapter and placed my finger by the verse.

"What does it mean when it says gift of God?" Chris queried.

"The verse says that the wages of sin is death. But God does not want us to remain in our sin. He wants us to know Him and has promised us the gift of eternal life if we place our faith in His provision, His Son Jesus Christ. The Bible says if you seek God and want a relationship with Him, you'll find him."

"I'm not sure what I want," replied Chris. "I don't like what I've done. I guess I want to start fresh with a new beginning if I can."

"That's a good place to start. You've recognized the sin in your life. Would you like to be forgiven of that sin?"

"That would be great, but I've already done all that stuff and can't take it back."

"There's something you must understand," I said slowly.

"I'm listening."

"God is the only one who can help us. We must want help and recognize our need for Him and the provisions He has made for us to be in a right relationship with Him. We must believe in Him and by faith receive all that He has to offer."

"Faith?"

"Faith is believing in something that you can't see, feel, or touch. It's taking God at His Word! Chris, do you believe in God?"

"Yes, I believe there's a God, but I know very little about these things."

"That's good! We believe there is a God by faith. God the Father knew we as humans were in trouble. He did something drastic to rescue us."

"What did he do?"

"He sent his Son into the world. Look here in John 3:16. Read what it says."

Chris read the verse out loud. "For God so loved the world that he gave his one and only Son, that whoever believes in him shall not perish but have eternal life."

"Now turn to Luke 1:35 and read that," I instructed.

Chris found the book, turned to the first chapter, and read verse 35.

"The angel answered, 'The Holy Spirit will come on you, and the power of the Most High will overshadow you. So the holy one to be born will be called the Son of God.' I know the Christmas story."

"It's more than a story. Jesus is God's provision: a perfect sinless sacrifice for our sins so that we might have forgiveness of sins and receive the promise of eternal life. In Romans 5:8, it says that God demonstrates his own love for us in this: While we were still sinners, Christ died for us. Jesus had to die to save us!"

"How did He save us?"

"God is just and holy! He had to punish sin. Because we are sinners, we should die for our sins. Jesus came to earth to die in our place. He took the hit! His innocent blood atoned for our sins. God the Father allowed His Son to pay for our sins. The Bible says that without the shedding of blood there is no forgiveness of sin and without faith it is impossible to please God. I want you to look up those two verses. Look up Hebrews 9:22 and Hebrews 11:6."

Chris looked up Hebrews 9:22 and read it right away.

"In fact, the law requires that nearly everything be cleansed with blood, and without the shedding of blood there is no forgiveness."

Without hesitation, Chris found Hebrews 11:6 and read it to me, "And without faith it is impossible to please God, because anyone who comes to him must believe that he exists and that he rewards those who earnestly seek him."

"We must believe that Jesus, the Son of God, willingly sacrificed Himself by being crucified on a cross where He shed His blood to pay our debt in full for all our sins, so that we might have forgiveness of our sins. He was a perfect sacrifice offered up once for all, so that we might know God the Father and live with Him eternally."

"That's amazing, Tom. I've never heard that before!" Chris replied.

Chris was listening with his whole heart and tracking with everything I was saying. We had been talking for an hour. The Apostle Paul's name kept coming up, and Chris wanted to know more about him. I turned to the book of Acts, which is the story of how the church began. Chris seemed very captivated by Paul. Paul's travels and experiences fascinated Chris and he wanted more. First he read a chapter, then I read another chapter, and we proceeded like that and read through all 28 chapters of the book of Acts! Chris said he identified with Paul because he sounded like a crazy man just like him. I could see the excitement in Chris's face, but I still hadn't asked him if he wanted to begin following Jesus like the Apostle Paul did.

"Let's go outside and sit in my backyard," I suggested. It was a pleasant evening with a cool breeze. We sat down under my maple tree and continued our conversation. I was amazed at what followed.

"Do you believe all the things we've been talking about?" Chris questioned.

"Yes, I do, Chris! There's a part of me you know nothing about, too. We've had a good friendship for seven years, but unless you see this side of me, our friendship wouldn't be complete."

"What do I have to do, Tom, to have what you have? Do I have to go to the priest and climb into the confessional and tell that guy what I've told you?"

"No, Chris," I said with a half-smile on my face. "God doesn't want you to be wrapped up in the rules and regulations of a religion. He wants a relationship with you just like we have with each other...but even better! He wants you to know Him and follow His Son Jesus who came into this world to make His Father known. Jesus said in John 14:6, 'I am the way and the truth and the life. No one comes to the Father except through me.' Are you interested in having this relationship?"

"Yes!" Chris responded exuberantly.

"It takes faith to believe, and Romans 10:17 tells us that faith comes from hearing the message, and the message is heard through the word about Christ. I've tried to tell you the best I can from what I've learned. If you believe what I've told you and what the Bible says, maybe you're ready to become a believer in Jesus Christ."

"I'm ready!" Chris replied.

"Chris, this isn't a game. I don't want you to do something to please me. It is by far the most important decision you will ever make because it reaches into eternity. If you truly believe that Jesus is God and that He died in your place for your sins, that He was buried, and that He rose from the dead, then the Bible says you will be saved."

"Tom, I believe. Tell me what I have to do."

"You've already done it."

"What do you mean?"

"You believe! John 6:29 says that the work of God is this: to believe in the one He has sent. And that's Jesus!"

"That's it?"

"Well, you also have to receive the gift that's been offered to you. In Romans 10: 8-11, your new friend Paul wrote this: 'The word is near you; it is in your mouth and in your heart,' that is, the message concerning faith that we proclaim: If you declare with your mouth, 'Jesus is Lord,' and believe in your heart that God raised him from the dead, you will be saved. For it is with your heart that you believe and are justified, and it is with your mouth that you profess your faith and are saved. As Scripture says, 'Anyone who believes in him will never be put to shame.' Chris, are you ready to do that?"

"I'm so ready, Tom."

"Alright, Chris, then repeat this prayer after me.

'Dear God, I believe You exist. I believe You sent Your Son Jesus to rescue me. I believe Jesus died in my place and paid for my sins on the cross. Forgive me now of my sin and come into my life. Give to me Your Holy Spirit to help me live for You and no longer for myself. In Jesus's name, I pray. Amen!'"

Chris prayed that prayer with me to receive Christ into his life. He never shut his eyes! He looked into my eyes with the most sincere look I have ever seen. There were no tears. I welcomed him into the family of God with a huge hug. Little did I know or realize what impact this decision would have on both of our lives.

Then Chris exclaimed, "I want two things. First, I want to get where you're at in your faith in half the time it took you to get there. Secondly, I want to be like this big ol' oak tree and bear fruit and have thousands of acorns!"

"Those are good requests, but it's not easy living a Christian life and being Christ-like in this world. In many ways, life as a Christian is much more difficult than your life before, but it's also way more rewarding. Only time will tell how you mature and how much fruit you will have in your life. And besides, this is not an oak tree. It's a maple. But let's pretend it's an oak tree. I like metaphors!"

Every question I asked Tom that night, he answered by opening up the Bible and turning to various parts of it for his answers. Everything he spoke and read from the Bible made perfect sense to me. I wholeheartedly gave myself to Jesus, who took the guilt of my sin away. Jesus replaced my guilt with pure joy through the forgiveness of all my sins and the knowledge that eternity exists over death's horizon for all who believe. My friend Jay's death turned my life upside-down and inside-out for a time. Jesus's death turned my life around for eternity...an eternity in which I may see my friend Jay once again. The guilt I had been carrying was suddenly lifted as I prayed with Tom. That guilt was transformed into joy.

When I left Tom's house at 2:15 a.m., I was riding on cloud nine with a smile on my face and a new Spirit in my soul. I felt relieved, happy, and content all at the same time. It felt like something I had been searching for in all the wrong places

was finally found. I would describe it as a peace that passes all understanding.

Discipleship

The Lord was working in my life and preparing me to help Chris in his newfound faith. After Chris received the gospel message and experienced God's forgiveness, he needed to grow in his walk with Jesus, his new friend.

I struggled in my faith journey to establish a personal quiet time with God. I always had good intentions, but I was never able to be consistent until I was held accountable.

During a leader's meeting for Bible Study Fellowship, I heard a talk on having a personal quiet time. In our Saturday morning meeting, we had a speaker whose name was Gary. He was telling us about his faith journey. He told us, "If you strip me down and take everything away from me, the last thing I will give up is my personal quiet time!"

With that statement, I sat straight up and he had my full attention.

"I don't know how I lived the Christian life without a quiet time. Actually, I know how I did... I didn't!" remarked Gary.

Gary held up a paperback devotional book. He opened it up and told us that the book had short paragraphs of Scripture on each page with lines underneath for journaling. Then he stated, "If you do something for 30 days in a row, you become familiar with the habit. If you do something for 60 days, you'll probably have a habit for life."

After the meeting, I approached Gary.

"I want what you have!" I told him passionately.

"You can have this devotional. It has a small portion of Scripture for each day. Read it and write your thoughts on the blank lines. I'll call you in 30 days to see how you're doing," he replied.

Gary was true to his word and he called me after 30 days.

"Hi Tom, how are you doing with your quiet time?"

I answered, "I did 16 out of 30 days."

"That's progress. I'll call you in 30 days," he responded.

I felt bad that I didn't do 30 days in a row, so I disciplined myself during the next 30 days. After 60 days, Gary called me again and asked me how I did. I was pleased to report that I had done 30 days in a row.

"Gary, thank you for holding me accountable. Having a daily quiet time has been amazing and I enjoy talking to God, reading His word, and making Him the main priority in my life," I told him excitedly.

"I'm grateful that I was able to help you establish this very important tool in your life. I am sure that now, your quiet times will become essential to your walk with the Lord."

He was right! Do something for 60 days in a row, and you will have a habit. We are creatures of habit, so why not work at establishing good habits? Today, I can honestly say I do not leave my house without spending time with

God. Establishing a personal quiet time made me ready and able to help Chris in his own walk with the Lord. You can't give someone what you don't have yourself.

I went to Northwestern Christian Bookstore and bought the same devotional that Gary had recommended to give to Chris. It was very helpful for me to have a tool to use in my newly established quiet time, so I figured it would be helpful to Chris as well.

Jesus had 12 disciples during His ministry time here in this world. Each of the 12 disciples had other men they were discipling. This has happened all through the ages, one man teaching another man what they have experienced in their walk with Jesus Christ. One could say that Bob Glockner discipled Denny McGuire, then Denny McGuire discipled Tom Hall, and Tom Hall discipled me. These men are my spiritual mentors. I knew all three, but benefited through Tom who discipled me directly. Through all discipling relationships, both men benefit spiritually. Proverbs 27:17 says, "As iron sharpens iron, so one person sharpens another."

We have a teacher and an example in Jesus Christ. We don't hold each other up on a pedestal, because we each have placed Jesus there. Our common pursuit is to know Him and know Him more fully than we did yesterday. Jesus said in John 17:17, "Sanctify them by the truth; your word is truth."

Therefore, a believer can't mature apart from growing in his or her understanding of God's Word. There's another verse that very accurately reflects what man-to-man discipleship is. 1 Thessalonians 2:8 says, "...so we cared for you. Because we

loved you so much, we were delighted to share with you not only the gospel of God but our lives as well."

I never once remember opening a Bible during the first 22 years of my life. The very first time I ever opened a Bible and purposely wanted to read something from it was that day Tom gave me a Bible for a graduation gift. Tom's gift led me to find and read Revelation 3:20. God used that one verse to turn my life towards Him and called me to become His disciple. Later I went to Tom, who became the man God used to introduce me to Jesus and to share with me how my sins could be forgiven through what He did on the cross. God was working in both of our hearts. Previously, God equipped Tom so that he could help me when God turned me in my tracks. Tom had been praying for me for six years, asking God to help me come to know His Son, Jesus. God answers prayers! And when God answers the prayers we utter, it fills us with great joy, since we know that He was the one who answered our prayers. I can only imagine how Tom felt when I knelt outside of his house and prayed to ask Jesus to forgive me of my sins and to take control of my life. After having prayed so diligently for me, Tom got to watch God directly answer his prayers right in his very own backyard!

It was one of the most incredible days in my life. I was thrilled when you made the decision to follow Jesus. I knew it was real and I thanked God for answering my prayers. I was a messenger, but God was the one who saved you and to Him we give all the glory! I was so excited for you and I knew that the angels in heaven were rejoicing with me as well!

Chris came over to my house one day and I told him how difficult it was for me to have a consistent time with the Lord every day. I told him about Gary's prayer for me and the way he kept me accountable. I gave Chris the devotional and challenged him to use it each morning for 60 days in a row.

"Chris, let's do the devotional together today," I said as I handed him the paperback book. The Scripture for the day was Colossians 1:9-14. I had Chris read the paragraph as I followed along in my Bible. It was about prayer, knowledge, wisdom, and understanding. We had to summarize this paragraph in our own words and then apply it in our lives.

Tom and I dove right into discipleship as Tom just described above. He gave me a NavPress publication entitled: "Devotional Diary: Scripture Reading Program No. 1." It had an introduction on how to use the plan that involved seven suggestions to help you develop a daily walk with the Lord as you fed on His Word. I was like a baby who was just learning to roll over. I had to be spoon-fed and the "Devotional Diary" was a perfect tool to help me get going with God. It taught me to plan in advance the best time to have a devotion and to place myself away from distractions.

At home during the first summer before starting my teaching career, I would often lock myself in the bathroom to have a devotional time away from all the other members of my family. I learned to prepare my heart in the first moments of my devotional time by simply praying, "Lord, open my eyes that I might see wondrous things out of your Word." The plan had

passages of Scripture listed to read for each day of the month for the whole year, all nicely laid out for anyone to follow. They were intentionally short to encourage you to mediate on what you read and identify what it was the Lord was trying to speak into your heart. This resource taught me to pin down the main thought of each of the passages, put my own title on the section, and record my thoughts in the journal. I was encouraged to meditate on these thoughts within the greater context of the verses, which caused me to read even more of the Word. This helped safeguard my mind from misinterpreting the passage.

The final things Tom taught me through this "Devotional Diary" had to do with profit and prayer. I learned that I profited from God by applying what I learned from His Word to my daily life. Personal application was accomplished by stating how my thoughts about the passage could help me be more like Jesus. In any given passage, I might come across a new revelation about Jesus, a promise I could claim, a command to obey, an example to follow, a sin to forsake, or an error to avoid. Finally, I learned to commit my application to the Lord in prayer with the realization that it is only by His power that we really will be changed from day to day. I learned to love the Word of God and spend time thinking about it and trying to apply it to my life in a meaningful way.

Tom and I worked daily in this "Devotional Diary" from June 27, 1979 (we began about a month after I committed my life to Jesus Christ) through August 22, 1981. It was a little over two years. We filled two of the books with our thoughts and shared our writings with each other often. Once in a while, we would swap books for a few days and write in each other's journals, then come back together and share with each other

what we wrote. I went 81 days without missing a day. Then I missed two days, did four days, and missed another day. I guess this really made me feel bad because I was doing it with Tom and I had to show him my empty days when I missed. I went another 258 days straight before missing again. There's a lot to be said about accountability.

Through all this, Tom and the Lord helped me establish the habit of having a morning devotional time, which is what Tom likes to call a "quiet time." This time before the Lord is a necessity in my life and continues to be the bedrock practice by which I try to start each day. I let my guard down once in a while due to traveling for ministry or family commitments, but I always come back to this time before the Lord in His Word: writing down my thoughts, praying, and thanking Him for the goodness, mercy, and grace He has extended towards me.

Chris and I met at least once a week. We shared our personal devotions with each other. Eventually, we did our devotions alone and then shared them with each other whenever we met. We prayed for each other's personal prayer requests. We used little cards with verses on them to help us memorize the Word. It was a tool called the Topical Memory System that The Navigators published. We had to say the reference, then say the verse from memory, and then say the reference again. This helped us memorize the verse and know where to find it in the Bible. We did all these things because I wanted Chris to become solid in his faith journey.

With these disciplines, we held each other accountable and grew in our spiritual strength. Besides establishing his own personal walk with the Lord, I wanted Chris to be passionate about man-to-man discipleship.

Earlier in my life, I had been discipled by an older man who introduced me to the Design for Discipleship Series (DFD) by the Navigators. Going through DFD really helped me get into God's Word, and I knew it would benefit Chris as well. Over the course of about two years, Chris and I went through all seven DFD books together. Each book is designed to strengthen your faith and knowledge of the Bible. It was thought-provoking material and challenged both of us. Because of this study, both of us were inspired to disciple one man a year for the rest of our lives. I see DFD as a multiplication tool! Over the years we've known each other, Chris and I have individually discipled many other men. The neat thing about this series is that once you've worked through it and completed all seven books, you don't have to prepare anymore because you've already completed each book. As you take another man through them, you can then focus more on the man in front of you and benefit from the insights the Lord gives that man.

We graduated to the Design for Discipleship Series and together went through all seven books in the series. I enjoyed this change of pace, but I kept on doing my own daily devotional time as we worked through the books. The titles of the books help describe the content Tom and I studied together as we worked through each book:

Book One: Your Life in Christ

Book Two: The Spirit-Filled Follower of Jesus

Book Three: Walking with Christ
Book Four: The Character of a Follower of Jesus
Book Five: Foundations of Faith
Book Six: Growing in Discipleship
Book Seven: Our Hope in Christ, Analysis of First Thessalonians

The last book in the series involved doing a Bible study of the book of 1 Thessalonians. These books took Tom and me into the third and fourth years of our discipleship relationship. Sometime along the way, my friend Tom went from being the leader of our discipleship time to being my mentor. I was fortunate to have a few different men invest their time and energy into my life as well, while Tom continued to be my main mentor as I got into more extensive ministry sharing the gospel message through EPPIC Ministries International, Inc.

When Tom and I first started in on using the "Devotional Diary," Tom also invited me to attend Bible Study Fellowship (BSF). He invited me to come to his house on Monday evenings and have dinner with him and his family before going to Brooklyn Center Covenant Church where BSF was held. I started BSF as an attendee beginning in September 1979. They were studying the first book in the Bible, Genesis. According to Genesis 1:1, "In the beginning God created the heavens and the earth."

Everything was a "new beginning" for me: coming to know Jesus, reading Scripture, prayer, and a whole lot of Bible study. I began listening to a man named Denny McGuire, who was the lay teaching leader for this BSF group of about 200 men. I was very moved in my spirit the first time I heard two hundred men belt out "Crown Him with Many Crowns" from the depths of their hearts. It was a booming, melodic experience, the likes of which I had never heard before. Sometime during my BSF days and my time with Tom, I moved in my infant faith from rolling over to learning how to crawl and then to walk with the Lord and finally, how to feed myself. I desired the meat of the truth of God's word and not just the milk of His Word. At some point in our Christian faith, we must move from being babes in Christ to being mature believers in Christ who are able to accurately handle the Word of truth and be found adequate and equipped for every good work. The one being discipled eventually becomes the one doing the discipling! The Lord multiplies Himself though it all as He equips His past, present and future disciples through His Word and the power of the Holy Spirit to accomplish His good, pleasing, and perfect will.

Our Ministry and Chris's Baptism

Shortly after Chris's conversion, he began attending my church. I was attending Northbrook Christian Missionary Alliance Church at that time.

"Chris, maybe we should volunteer for some ministry at our church," I suggested.

"What do you have in mind, Tom?"

"Since we're both teachers, I was thinking we could teach a Sunday school class."

"I'm game! How would we go about doing that?" Chris asked.

"We could approach our pastor and ask him if he needs any help with the Sunday school morning classes."

So that's what we did. We made an appointment with our pastor and met him in his office during the week. The pastor said there was a need for someone to teach our high school students. We were open to his suggestion and agreed to teach them. Our plan was to go through some of Paul's letters from the Bible with the students.

We got together and planned to begin with them in the letter to the Galatians. We prepared the material and began teaching the following Sunday morning.

As the students filed into the room that first morning, they were surprised to see Chris and me.

I looked back in my journals about teaching Sunday school with Tom at Northbrook. I have a list of 31 names of high school students we taught on Sunday and Wednesday nights.

"Hi! I'm Tom Hall. I have attended Northbrook for the past few years and this is my friend, Chris. We will be your teachers for the coming year."

"Hi, I'm Chris Erickson. Tom and I have been friends for a few years. We are excited to be your teachers this year. We both teach in the public school system. We are not allowed to share our faith with our students and are excited to share and study God's word with you in the church!"

I began by asking them to open their Bibles to Galatians chapter one. They did not all have Bibles, so I suggested they share with a friend as I read the chapter. After reading the chapter, Chris and I led a discussion on each paragraph. The students were reluctant to get involved and it was difficult to get their attention. After our first encounter, Chris and I were amazed at their disinterest.

We tried to make our presentations interesting. We shared our testimonies and used illustrations.

One Sunday morning as I began teaching, one of the students turned his back to me and began reading a magazine. I told him to turn around and face me. Reluctantly, he slowly turned around with a scowl on his face.

"What did I ever do to you to make you so disrespectful towards me?" I questioned.

"I have nothing against you!"

"That's not what it looks like to me!" I responded. The rest of the class quietly watched our dialogue. "Why do you come to this class anyway?"

"I'm only here for one reason. My father makes me come. I hate coming to church."

"I'm sorry about that, but if you can't be respectful, maybe we can find some other place for you to spend your time."

This was the extent of the conversation. He continued to come and at least showed me some respect. However, the problem wasn't just him. Most of the students were not interested in the Bible or what we had to say. However, there were a few students who were very interested and that's what kept us going.

I wrote in my journals about students who responded to our teaching and the gospel message. A few came to know the Lord, teaching me that just because you go to church doesn't necessarily mean you have a relationship with Jesus. There were others with honest questions and serious doubts that surfaced after we got to know them and spent some time with them. All the challenging behaviors Tom and I experienced were typical of high school students who are in the throes of developing physically, mentally, and emotionally as they seek to discover their own

identity and become their own person. Tom and I stepped into a group of students who were looking for affirmation and needed to be loved, listened to, and accepted. Spiritually, they were all over the map. We prayed for them and committed our time and energy to them. God gave us both the grace to hang in there with them and teach as we felt He was directing us to teach.

Chris was single and had more time on his hands. He met with some of the students individually throughout the week and won some of them over.

It's called bribery. I challenged the high school students to attend the class and do the lessons. I told the students that if they did that and had perfect attendance, those who did would get to do something special at the end of the school year. Six students embraced that challenge and had perfect attendance. I had a friend who had a small plane. I arranged for the students and myself to fly down to Rochester, have lunch at the airport, and then fly back to Flying Cloud Airport in Eden Prairie. One of the students enjoyed it so much that he eventually did everything he had to do to obtain his pilot's license. He was in the news one year when he had to land a malfunctioning single engine plane on a local city street!

As Tom and I became more involved as Bible Study Fellowship (BSF) leaders, we fulfilled our commitment to teaching the high school Sunday school class. We did not continue due to the time constraints both of us had serving in BSF. God was at work during our time teaching high school students. I would love to know the outcome of each of the lives we encountered.

As Chris was attending our church, he began to get interested in baptism.

"Tom, do you think I should get baptized?"

"Chris, that's your call. Why don't you pray about it and look at some Scripture verses before you make a decision?"

"I was baptized as an infant in the Catholic church, but I don't remember that."

Chris searched the Scriptures and prayed about it for a few weeks. He was diligent in his search. Finally, he came to his decision.

"Tom, I've decided to get baptized. It's an important step in my faith journey. I want the world to know I'm serious about my commitment to God. It symbolizes my love for Him. When I go under the water, my old life comes with me and dies. When I am lifted up, it represents who I am now in Christ. The old has gone and the new has come."

"I support your decision! I was baptized when I was twelve. I'm not sure I understood its significance then, but I do now," I told him.

About a month later, we had a baptismal service at our church. Chris and three older women went through instructions explaining the importance of water baptism. Water baptism does not save you, but it is evidence that you want to follow and serve Christ.

My family and I were there to support Chris and his decision to be baptized. When it was his turn, our pastor dunked him completely under the water. When he came up, he gave a triumphal shout! After the service was over, we had a celebration in our home for him. I asked Chris why he shouted after he came up out of the water. "It was not half as loud as I wanted to shout, Tom," was his response. Chris was definitely on his way in his new life in Christ.

I did come up out of the water with a whoop and a holler! I went back to Northbrook years later with EPPIC where we presented the gospel message through mime. A person came up to me at the end of the presentation and said, "Aren't you Chris Erickson? I remember you. You're the guy who came out of the baptismal with a whoop and a holler that startled everyone present, but it also made us smile and laugh."

"Yep, I'm the guy," I said with a smile.

Our Teaching Careers

The phone rang and I answered.

"Tom, this is Chris calling. I have some good news!"

"What is it, Chris?"

"I interviewed for a teaching position a couple of days ago. I felt the interview went well. Today I got a call from the principal at Forest Hills Elementary school. He congratulated me and said I was hired to teach fifth grade this fall at his school."

"That's great news, Chris! We're both teaching fifth grade now. We can compare notes and pray for one another. Why don't you come over to my house this Friday for dinner, and we can work on some strategies for setting up your classroom. I can answer any questions you might have. I'm excited for you! You're going to have a great career."

The following Friday, Chris came over to my house. Sandy fixed a great dinner. My kids were excited for Chris as well. Mike was eleven years old and Katie was nine years old. They were both about the age of Chris's future students. After dinner, we went out to my screened-in porch and talked.

"Now, instead of paying for school, you will be receiving a check. That'll be quite a switch for you, won't it?" I asked.

"I guess so! I'm supposed to be in school the week before the kids come. They call it teacher's workshop. What's that all about?" asked Chris.

"Workshop is when all the staff comes together at the beginning of the year. It's led by the school principal. You will meet all your colleagues. Your principal will discuss goals and strategies for the new school year. You also get a chance to meet your fifth-grade team. They will be a great help to you in the coming year. You'll get to know them very well because you'll be working closely with each of them. Your fifth-grade team will have a leader and will discuss the curriculum that you will use the coming year. They will also answer any questions you might have. After the meetings are over, you will have time to set up your room and get ready for the students to come and have a great experience with you. You will need to make your room look like a classroom, inviting your students to enjoy a great year."

"Any suggestions on setting up my classroom?"

"Get a set of alphabetical letters. I would put them around the top of your classroom…it gives a nice classroom effect. You'll also make all your bulletin boards. Try to make them colorful with good messages and something that they could look at and enjoy."

"I'll enjoy setting up my classroom. I want my students to feel it will be an exciting place to learn, grow personally, and advance academically."

"I actually don't enjoy setting up my classroom, Chris. Every year, Sandy does it for me. She loves doing that stuff. My classroom comes alive after she is finished. All the other teachers in my school rush around because they don't feel they have enough time to set up. I get a cup of coffee and go around and get all caught up with my colleagues after the summer."

You sluggard.

"It's Sandy's great gift to me! It helps me to get ready for another year and be relaxed. Our staff has been together for many years, and I've made some good friends that I teach with."

"What about the curriculum?" asked Chris with a questioning look on his face.

"When you meet with your team, they'll help you out in this area. I don't know if you will be team teaching or self-contained. They'll let you know that when you get together. Don't be afraid to ask questions because this is a new beginning for you and that's how you learn."

"What subjects will I be teaching?"

"If your grade level is self-contained, you'll be teaching all the subjects."

"How will that go?"

"You'll find out when you have your first meeting with your fifth-grade team. After you set up your classroom and arrange your desks, then you can look at the teacher's manuals for the subjects you have to teach. The manuals do a good job of helping you understand how to present lessons for that subject. But don't be afraid to be creative and follow your own way of teaching any particular lesson."

"Where will I find the manuals?"

"They will be in your classroom," I told him. "I would set up your desks in rows at first. Start out very traditional. You can change your seating arrangement many times throughout the course of the year. I would suggest that you go over your class list and orally pronounce each name. Then make name tags and put them on each desk. Mix up the boys and girls. After that, place all the textbooks you're going to use on top of their desks. When they come in that first day, stand at the door, shake their hands and welcome them with a big smile on your face. Their first impressions of you will be very important!"

"You mean I shouldn't wait 'till after Christmas to smile?" Chris said teasingly.

"Funny, Chris. That was a bit of advice I should have never listened to when I first started teaching."

I continued to give Chris suggestions for the first day of school.

"When they've entered your classroom, ask them to find their desk, which they can locate in the classroom with their name tag on it. Let them know that you're in control and are excited to be their teacher."

"What about my responsibility to teach all subjects?" Chris queried.

"Look through the teacher's manuals on each subject. Just skim them and look at the units you're going to teach."

"That seems kind of overwhelming!"

"It is, in a way! This is your first year, so each day will be a new day. It will not always go perfectly as you teach your students. You will have good and bad days. All you need to do is stay a couple days ahead of your students and learn along with them. You'll probably be asked to make weekly lesson plans. That will help direct you each week. However, you must be flexible with your lesson plans and look for teachable moments. You don't know when they will come up, so don't be so tight with your lesson plans that you can't capture the moment when kids learn the best. Tell stories and use illustrations to make your learning fun and enjoyable. If you get frustrated, don't show it! Just smile and work through the lesson even if it's going really bad."

"I'm such a rookie, but I guess that's how all teachers start their careers."

"Chris, take your new faith with you. Pray for each of your students and shoot up prayers to God all day long. God will help you love these kids, answer their questions, and teach them. Make your classroom a place where each of them can grow and thrive. You can't use the Bible directly, but you can use its principles in your classroom every day. You have God's Holy Spirit in you and He will be a great resource for you all year. You also have the standards of the Bible that you can use. An example of this would be the definition of love as laid out in 1 Corinthians chapter 13."

We talked for a couple of hours. It was a great dialogue and every teacher should have this conversation when he or she begins their first year as a new teacher.

I was fortunate to gain wisdom from your experience as a public school teacher. Our discussions certainly opened my eyes to all that was expected of me as a classroom teacher and all that needed to be done at the beginning of the school year.

During this conversation, I also broke down how I managed the first day of school with my new class.

"It's important to get your class into a structure and routine. For the first 15 minutes of class, you should interact with them. I'd tell them a little story about who you are and how you feel about teaching. I'd tell them it's your honor to be their teacher. Then say, 'We're going to have a great year together.' You want them to get to know you and learn more about you. You want to earn their trust."

"It sounds like the first day is pretty important," Chris replied.

"It is! Even after teaching all these years, I still get the butterflies! When the students come into my classroom, they need to get organized for the day. They have about five minutes to do that. They need to organize their desk and sharpen their pencils and move their pins to indicate whether they're going to have a hot or cold lunch. At a certain time, let's say 8:35, they will all need to be in their desks ready for the day to begin. If they are not in their desks at the set time there will be a consequence."

You were really drilling down here. Details, details, details!

"During that first week, I will remind them if they were not in their desk at the proper time. I will give them some grace that first week. After that, their names will be on the board and they will have a consequence: 10 push-ups or 20 sit-ups. After two weeks and some consequences, they will all be in their seats on time and ready to go. This will help the routine and make the day go smoothly. The first fifteen minutes is an important time in the day. We salute the flag, say the Pledge of Allegiance, and have a sharing time. I encourage them to watch the news or read the paper. We will talk about current events first. After that, we will have personal sharing time. If something happened to me that day, I will share my little story. Eventually, the kids will really enjoy this time and we will get to know each other a lot better. It will also help them with their listening and speaking skills. They will be learning and not even realizing it."

I've experienced some of the best times of laughter during these sharing times with students. They have laughed at my stories and I have laughed at theirs. I used to love to question students about their stories and it often led to some very comical details that gave all who were listening a better yarn. I remember a third grader who was distraught one morning over losing a friend who was moving away to California. I encouraged him to tell his friend how he felt about her. He said he couldn't do that. When I asked why, he said, "Because she's a horse!" The class burst out laughing, as did I. The little boy, who told the story with tears in his eyes, saw the humor in it and laughed along with us.

"The next important thing to do with them is to set up boundaries. I draw a square on the board and ask them, 'What is this?' They answer by telling me that it is a square. 'It's more than a square. It's a box. What's inside the box?' I say. I draw a stick figure of a boy and a girl. Then I explain that there are fifth-graders in this box, but it's small and crowded. I open it up and make a bigger box around the smaller one. 'Now there's more room to move around,' I say.

"Then I explain that each line stands for guidelines or rules. The first line in this class is when we have a discussion they must raise their hand and not shout out. I will call on that individual and we will respect him or her by listening. If they are talking while someone else is speaking, they've crossed the line and there will be a consequence.

"The next line is that they cannot hurt anyone. This can be done physically or with words or notes. If they hurt someone, they've crossed the line.

"The next line is they cannot leave the classroom without my permission. They are my responsibility, and I want to know they are here or if they've asked permission to leave.

"The final line is that we must respect each other. I will always respect them and I want them to respect each other. If they disrespect someone, they've crossed the line and they will be disciplined. I decide the consequence.

"In the first couple of weeks if they cross the line, I will just point it out to them. If they continue to cross the line, they have to accept the consequences because they understood the boundaries and crossed them anyway. They know beforehand what I expect. I watch them closely and when they cross the line, I discipline them. After two or three weeks, they understand the limits and discipline becomes rather easy.

"They will test the boundaries! I will make sure to discipline anyone who crosses the line in that first couple of weeks. I don't need any more than these four rules. If they stay within the box, they will be in good shape. If they cross the line, there will be a consequence. It's as easy as that!" I told him.

I'm not sure if I used this as you laid it out, but I'm sure I used some form of discipline that involved consequences and positive reinforcement. My favorite system to affect student behavior revolved around the use of marbles and a marble jar. Fourth graders loved it!

Chris and I discussed our teaching styles. In some areas we are very much alike, and in other areas we are very different. We each had to learn to teach to our strengths. We talked often during the first year. Chris did a great job. As a classroom teacher, he was very gifted and creative. He was the kind of teacher students would never forget.

Does gifted and creative mean jumping from a standing position straight over a student's desk to the other side of it? It was impossible for a fourth grader to do this, try as they may. Would it be considered creative to turn a student's desk upside-down because they allowed it to get so messy you could not close it

or find anything that was needed in it? I would pick up the desk by its legs and turn it upside-down to let all its contents fall out onto the floor. The guilty student had to clean up and put their desk into order during recess time. Nobody wanted to get their desk sacked and have to give up their recess! Maybe building a stage in the classroom and then giving Paddington Bear plays for the K-3rd graders counts as gifted and creative. If these things qualify, then yeah…gifted and creative. Then there was the wax museum we did for Halloween. Fun stuff!

That's pretty creative, Chris. I won't explain all the wonderful and exciting units Chris taught, but his students loved him. One year, we decided we would like to exchange classrooms. We checked with our principals and they thought it was a great idea. We exchanged lesson plans and spent a day in each other's class. I enjoyed teaching Chris's students. I told stories about our relationship and had a very good day. Chris, on the other hand, had some tricks up his sleeve. He included some games and really turned my students on. They couldn't stop talking about him the next day.

Throughout our careers, we spent a lot of time talking shop. I feel that throughout our dialogue, we helped each other become more effective teachers. One discussion Chris and I had was about being a Christian teacher in the public school. We were at a coffee shop when I asked Chris a question.

"What impact can a Christian teacher have on his students?"

Right away the dialogue began.

"Tom, it's a wide-open field! We have kids from all walks of life for ten months, six and a half hours a day, five days a week," Chris said.

"You're right, Chris! They come to us in their formative years and we do a good job with the curriculum, but also teach principles and values."

"Tom, some of my students have never gone to church or opened a Bible. As a Christian, I am who I am in Christ. As a teacher, I can't leave who I am at the door to my classroom. My influence on my students is a result of who I am as a Christian teacher in the public school. As such, I desire to be a role model for my students that will help positively direct them over the course of their lifetime in all manner of ways."

"The book of Proverbs alone is filled with wisdom and knowledge and instruction that would benefit each student greatly, but the problem is that we can't share those truths," I said.

"I'm not so sure. When I share something from the truth of God's word, I don't have to identify it as such. Truth always has a way of finding its own way. When it's appropriate, I'm not afraid to use what I know from the Word of God to help give insight or understanding to one of my students. To my knowledge, the only thing we cannot and should not do is try to proselytize a student by trying to convince them to believe what we believe. I am there to educate a student towards being a good citizen of this country. That is my primary goal as a public school teacher. I would not want a public school teacher teaching my child about their beliefs. I consider that to be the parent's job."

"You're right, Chris, we have the truth and shouldn't be afraid to let it flow out of us. We can't tell our students about Jesus Christ in the classroom, nor should we. However, we have the standards of the Ten Commandments, the golden rule, and the Bible as our resources. We have the Holy Spirit within us, making our bodies temples of God. The Holy Spirit is our comforter, counselor, and teacher. Those are resources that unbelievers don't have. We can use these resources every day. God will help us become better teachers and love our kids with *agape* love: a love that expects nothing in return."

"That's great, Tom! We also have the power of prayer. I pray for my students and their families every day by name. I also pray for my principal and coworkers."

"You know what, Chris? God will also help us with our attitude in the teacher's lounge, strengthen us for each day, and help us impact those parents and students we come into contact with through the year."

"You're right. Every day in our classroom, we need to rely on the resources Jesus gives us and love our students," Chris responded.

"Let's hold each other accountable by checking with each other often. Let's agree to pray for each other every day."

I've always maintained that there is a big difference between being a teacher who happens to be a Christian and being a Christian teacher.

That's very true!

Chris loved his students and wanted to share the gospel with them during the school day. That was not allowed in the public school, which frustrated Chris. He tried to figure out something that he could do to overcome this hurdle. He decided to rent the school cafeteria and have a voluntary "Saturday School."

I'm not sure if this had ever been done before. Somehow, he pulled it off! Many students came and, with Chris's creativity, the kids had all kinds of great experiences during these Saturdays with their teacher. He invited me a couple of times, and I did yo-yo tricks and taught yo-yo skills. Each Saturday, Chris gave a story from the Bible and shared the gospel with the students.

Chris's administrator was not comfortable with what he was doing and called him into his office one day to address the matter. Chris stood his ground and told his principal that there was nothing wrong with what he was doing. When the meeting was over and as he was walking out of the principal's office, his principal told him that the district's lawyers were going to be taking a look at it. Chris left realizing that he was indirectly being pressured to stop doing what he was doing. But Chris pressed on, knowing there was no legal basis for making him discontinue this activity.

Despite Chris's reputation for being an excellent teacher, he experienced multiple instances where his principal and superintendent both tried to squelch his witness with respect to his faith. One principal even took it upon herself to remove a book about Billy Graham from the library's bookshelf claiming it was religious, but left books about other religions and occult things on the shelves.

To Chris's credit, he managed to walk a fine line between what a Christian teacher can do and what a Christian teacher shouldn't do within the public schools. Chris believed any teacher, himself included, was not there in the public school to proselytize a child. But he also firmly believed a Christian teacher can't leave his or her own beliefs at the door. If a student asked him about things related to his faith and/or beliefs, he would honestly answer them… and they did ask…and they do ask.

I believe most students are starving for the truth and don't realize it. When these young people hear the truth, it satisfies their souls. Students are fed a lot of contemporary thought that has no substance and often makes no sense. Theory is presented as truth and leaves students confused and hopeless. The Scriptures offer answers to questions that satisfy the soul, affirm the value of each student, and create purpose and hope for this life and the promise of eternity that only God rightfully offers.

Toward the end of Chris's teaching career, which spanned 15 years, he determined God had called him into a ministry to share Christ and the gospel around the world. This was a hard decision because he and his family enjoyed the security that a teaching career provided. Despite this, he answered God's call and that opened a new chapter in his life.

Chris's Calling

At the age of 22, the day after graduating from college on May 15, 1979, the Lord called me to Himself while crossing an open field reading Revelation 3:20. A month later, through my friend Tom Hall, I accepted Jesus Christ as my Lord and Savior. I started teaching elementary school right out of college and spent those first four years being discipled by Tom. I also was involved in Bible Study Fellowship in a variety of ways over the years. I attended BSF as a participant, then I served as a discussion leader, and I even took on the role of a class administrator at one point. I was involved in a men's class of 200 and a single young adult class of 450 at different times. All that took place over a period of eight years from 1979 to 1987. I grew in my knowledge of the word of God, in my career as a teacher, and as a witness to the reality of Jesus at work in my life.

In 1980, I traveled as a new believer for 72 days through Europe and North Africa. While standing on a beach on the island of Corfu in Greece, looking across to the Albanian coastline, the Lord spoke to my heart and told me I would be going there to share the gospel message. As a new believer, this experience both amazed and confused me. Could God really be speaking to me in such a way? I stood there on the beach surprised by what I thought I heard. My next thought was about how I might do such a thing. I then realized I had no idea how to do that and told the Lord that He would have to bring His will about if I was to do it. That's where I left that conversation with God, but I thought about it many times after returning from Europe.

After Chris's teaching career was well underway, he became involved with an organization called EPPIC Ministries International.

As Tom mentioned in the previous chapter, I started a program I called "Saturday School." I rented a space in the public school where I taught and shared my faith in Christ with students. I also invited students to participate in Saturday School by mailing an invitation to the students' parents. I was using this opportunity to get to know and witness to the parents of my students, especially their fathers. I did this for four years and experienced some fruit from this undertaking. During the first year of Saturday School, one of my students who knew Jesus led her friend to the Lord. Another special moment occurred when I invited an EPPIC Ministries mime team to come and do a Christmas presentation at Saturday School. I invited all my students and parents to this event and 45 kids and parents attended. The EPPIC crew presented a 45-minute mime presentation set to music that totally blew me away with their message of sound and silence. As I looked around at the audience, parents and students alike were in tears. It was a powerful presentation of the gospel message and my first exposure to EPPIC. Little did I realize then what a large part EPPIC would end up playing in my own faith journey.

In December 1983, I attended the Urbana Student Missions Convention. I drove the bus for Wooddale Church down to Urbana Champagne, Illinois, but was not registered for the conference. That was a problem. With close to 19,000 students attending the conference, there was no place to stay, so I slept the first night on the bus which was cold at that time of year. The next day, I just happened to run into an EPPIC mime team registering for the convention and registered with them as a tenth member on their nine-member team. The team was a combination of single young adults, high school students, and their director. The team graciously offered a place for me to stay off-campus in housing they had arranged for the team. They also asked me to be with them as they performed in the field house to roving students that would stop, hundreds at a time, to witness the gospel message being played out without saying a word. The team coaxed me out front after short presentations to speak for them, announcing to the audience who they were, where they were from and what they were doing at Urbana: recruiting students to serve within EPPIC full time. They even talked me into putting on white face makeup and an EPPIC performance shirt to play a small role in a sketch they did called "Toytime." I think at that point I was hooked on the ministry and the work they were accomplishing for the Lord. I purposed to connect with them in January when I returned from the convention.

On the bus ride back from the Urbana Missions Convention, the Lord called me through a set of circumstances to do the work of an evangelist and informed me I was going to a conference

for itinerant evangelists that was taking place in Amsterdam in 1986. Once again, I whispered within my being, "If it's Your will, You will accomplish it."

In January 1984, I began working with EPPIC Ministries International as a ministry team member sharing biblical truth through the performing art of pantomime. I also became a member of Wooddale Church in Eden Prairie, Minnesota, and began serving within the church in various capacities. I was 26 years old when I attended my first EPPIC rehearsal. Other than the director, I was the oldest one present. I resolved in my heart and mind to learn from this group and purposely did not take up any leadership role. I started performing just like any newbie did in a small role and in a limited capacity. I remember the first EPPIC presentation I was involved in. We were on an elevated stage with the stage lighting blinding me from knowing where the end of the stage dropped off. I thought for sure I was going to go tumbling off that stage into the darkness and end up in someone's lap. Thankfully, that didn't happen, and I made it safely on and off the stage a few times during that presentation.

Chris became a participant in EPPIC and not only enjoyed it, but was excellent at learning the skills necessary to play his roles.

One evening, EPPIC performed at my school for a group called Awana that met in the gym. I stayed after school that day to watch and see what Chris was into with this ministry. It was the first time I had seen their performance, and it was amazing! I watched as the elementary students in the audience were riveted on the performance.

The visual performance told stories from the Bible that were all strung together in a compelling way. It was clearly understood without any actor saying a word.

There was a scene in which Jesus was being whipped. A boy about four years old was sitting on his mother's lap. Tears were streaming down his face. He seemed to clearly understand the story that was being acted. EPPIC gave a 45-minute presentation. The audience was totally involved in the story as it was presented in pantomime by the performers. Chris played the role of Jesus, and I was really impressed by what I saw.

After the presentation, Chris shared the gospel verbally. He stated that Jesus died on a cross, was buried, and rose from the grave. Several students who watched the performance asked Jesus to come into their hearts. I was impressed at the unique way Bible stories were communicated to the audience. As I watched the performance, the powerful visual aspect left a lasting impression on my heart. To me it was like listening to ten sermons. I now understood why Chris, who loved Jesus so dearly, wanted to be a part of this group.

We presented the gospel locally in and around Minnesota. In 1984, we traveled to Australia and around the country.

While trying to get time off teaching to do a mission trip with my church to the Philippines in 1985, the Lord asked me a question: "Are you willing to give up everything I've given you to do exactly what I want you to do?" I thought, "You mean you want me to give up a five-year teaching experience to do a month-long mission trip to the Philippines?"

He just repeated the question: "Are you willing to give up everything I've given you to do exactly what I want you to do?" With much hesitation, fear, and trembling, I answered, "Yes."

Then He said, "That's all I wanted to know...keep teaching." The Lord seemed to be testing my willingness at that moment in time to do His will.

By 1986, I was learning to play the Satan role in EPPIC's sketch material. This role is a very important part of the presentations. I was also getting set to lead an EPPIC team on a tour through the Scandinavian countries. I co-led that team just after attending the Billy Graham Conference in Amsterdam for itinerant evangelists. God fulfilled His word that He gave to me back in 1984 on that bus ride home from Urbana-Champaign, Illinois, the day after the Urbana Student Missions Convention was over.

After we toured the Scandinavian countries, I served in EPPIC as a staff member and led teams on international mission trips. In 1990, I started serving within EPPIC as the organizations director and setting up the organization to engage in more extensive international evangelistic mission work.

In 1992, while standing on a hill overlooking a camp an EPPIC team was staying at during the 1992 Summer Olympics in Spain, I was contemplating and praying about whether it was worth it to leave my career to do evangelistic work.

I asked the Lord, "Is it worth it?"

His response was a simple "Yes."

In 1993, EPPIC was working on sending a mime crew back to Australia, but everything kept pulling us to Europe. God was fulfilling His word to me that He gave me while standing on a beach on the island of Corfu in 1980, while looking at the Albania coastline. Again, God fulfilled His word to me thirteen years later! By God's grace, EPPIC's mime ministry crew shared "The Gospel in Mime" in Croatia, Yugoslavia, Western Europe, and Albania. In Albania, we partnered with the Hellenic Missionary Union who owned and operated a 66-foot sail boat called the Morning Star. One night on that particular mission trip as I was in prayer aboard the Morning Star, I was overwhelmed with God's amazing love for the lost to the point that I could not handle the emotion of it. I felt it was a glance into the burden God carries to redeem His creation. That moment brought me to tears, tears that fueled the flames of my desire to share the gospel more and more.

I had another experience that happened to me in 1994 while flying into Jetta, Saudi Arabia. As the plane descended into Jetta's airport, I was overwhelmed with emotion that suddenly welled up inside of me. The emotions were so intense, they brought me to tears as I sat in my aisle seat. One of my team members asked me what was wrong, but all I could do was wave her off as I was barely able to speak. We landed and the passengers deplaned as I was still shaking emotionally. Even as officials came through the plane, these emotions still had a hold on me. I wonder if any of the officials noticed me sitting there in tears. I could not have explained it if I had been asked. The plane took to the skies again and at about the same point in elevation where I initially was overcome with emotion, the emotions lifted from me. I still do not know what His plans for me are with respect to this experience or that specific place in the world. I do know that the Lord used these experiences to soften my heart towards leaving my teaching career and following His leading to do the work of an evangelist.

Through these experiences, I sensed the Lord calling me to full-time ministry and was led to leave my teaching career in 1995 to focus on evangelistic work through EPPIC. That same year, I was commissioned for missionary service through Woodale Church. I currently serve as one of Woodale's Global Partners.

After 15 years as a classroom teacher, Chris resigned his teaching position and became a full-time leader in EPPIC. Chris had already met his wife at this point in time, as she was also a participant in EPPIC. He supported his family through people who gave financially each month to the ministry. I supported Chris's ministry, and as my children got married, both of them supported Chris as well.

I remember having this conversation with Chris after he made the decision to leave teaching in order to fully pursue mission work through EPPIC.

"Tom, I've decided to leave education after this year and go into ministry full time."

"Really? That's a pretty big decision, Chris."

"I've prayed about it, and God is leading me to share the gospel. I feel like my hands are tied in the public school classroom."

"Chris, how can you give up your salary, benefits, and retirement?" I asked, surprised.

"I know," he said. "But my wife is on board, and I really think this is what God wants me to do."

"I trust you, Chris, and more importantly I trust God. If He's called you, which I believe He has, He will always provide."

Though quitting his job was a drastic decision, God always provided what Chris and his family needed. Chris set up a board of people to help organize his ministry and keep him accountable. Eventually, I became a member of the board, which put me behind the scenes and provided me with an opportunity to support Chris in a tangible way.

EPPIC stands for Each Person Personally In Christ. They are a traveling team of evangelists who share the gospel locally, nationally, and internationally through mime. They train teams around the world to do the same. Chris has trained mime ministry crews in Ukraine, Guatemala, Honduras, Bulgaria, and the United States. EPPIC trains the teams in mime technique and EPPIC sketch material, then supplies the costumes, mime make-up kits, and equipment needed to be a fully functional mime ministry crew.

Though I never traveled with Chris, I supported him, prayed for him, and helped him train the leaders. It was not a cakewalk for him. As his friend, it was challenging for me to watch him go through some difficult times. There was opposition and people doubted that the ministry would survive, but I kept reminding everyone what a heart for the Lord Chris had and that God had never let us down in the past. I used my influence as a friend to help the others understand his strong faith and wise judgment. I served on the board for 15 years.

Working in cross-cultural ministry, I am most surprised by how the Lord chooses to do His work differently in different places to reach people, establish His church, and equip those who

believe. There's no cookie cutter form to use, no one template to apply. As a teacher, I learned to monitor and adjust within the classroom environment to best meet my students' needs. In ministry, I've learned to be flexible, walk humbly, and work cooperatively without letting my own expectations or needs create anxiety for anything I'm trying to accomplish. These patterns have served me well within the cross-cultural work I've been doing these past thirty-five years and have helped me deal with all the surprises along the way. I have traveled all over the world sharing the gospel with tens of thousands of people in many different cultures. Mime has created opportunities to creatively share the gospel, often where opportunities didn't originally exist.

I attribute all that has been accomplished to the Lord and His goodness, mercy, and loving-kindness. I realize that apart from Him, I can do nothing. He is my strength and my ever-present help in and through all things, good and bad. It is a privilege to be able to serve Jesus in this way, traveling around the world and experiencing so much of His creation and the ministry of His church. It is a humbling experience to serve Jesus Christ.

With respect to my family, seeing my three daughters receive Jesus Christ and grow in their walk with Him, despite a divorce and especially in the face of what missionary kids already go through, is from my perspective a great ministry success. I can only attribute this success and the faith of my daughters to the grace, mercy, and love of the Lord.

Regarding ministry, what I enjoy most in all that God does is seeing and experiencing one more person come to know Him. Next, I love it when He helps people grow in their faith and live it out in their daily lives. I take great pleasure in witnessing others use "The Gospel in Mime" without my help. The development and multiplication of EPPIC mime crews nationally and in other countries has been a very rewarding and satisfying experience. The scriptural call surrounding The Great Commission is clear, laid out in Matthew 28:18-20. As a believer in Jesus Christ, I am called to follow the command of Jesus to "go and make disciples of all nations, baptizing them in the name of the Father and of the Son and of the Holy Spirit, and teaching them to obey everything I have commanded you." Jesus's instruction is given with the promise that He will be with us always, even "to the very end of the age." All glory and praise to God, because He is the one who works in us to accomplish His will as we pursue the ways in which He calls us in this life.

By far, the hardest thing I've had to overcome in ministry has been the stigma and the lingering effects of divorce. Other ministry challenges include the constant financial pressures, which create difficult circumstances that are challenging to navigate on a tight budget, and team dynamics or situations with individuals that go awry and become public. These situations have been a source of stress and required much effort to work through, overcome, and move past. Working with performing art ministry crews is always interesting and challenging.

I continue working in and through EPPIC to fulfill our vision to use "The Gospel in Mime" tool more extensively and strategically. Through this organization, the gospel message of Jesus Christ has been shared with thousands upon thousands in countries all over the world. Though the work of the ministry has been challenging, it is always rewarding to see another

individual place their faith in Jesus and know that the Lord used me in that process. It is a humbling experience when you know who it is that you serve.

Attacks from the Enemy

When I said "yes" to serve God in BSF, little did I know the battle that would take place in my life as well as the life of my family. At first, the responsibility was overwhelming. With Sandy's help, I was able find a way to function successfully.

However, I did not anticipate the struggle in the unseen world. Satan did not like the decision that I made to serve the Lord and the impact it would have on many men who were becoming serious about their faith journey. With God's help, I was able to recruit teams of men over my ten years of serving in BSF who supported and prayed for me and my family. Their prayers were powerful and helped in many ways, some of which I'm not even aware of.

The first attack from the enemy concerned my career. As a fifth-grade teacher, our team would take students on a field trip to an environmental center for a period of one week. It was during one of these trips that my colleague was accused of improperly touching a student. I did not believe the accusation because I had worked with this gentleman for many years. However, as I pursued the inquiry, I realized that something serious had happened. We removed the teacher from any contact with the students for the rest of the week. We contacted our superintendent, finished out the week, and returned to the cities. My colleague was taken home by another teacher. When I arrived at our school, the superintendent was there to confront me. He was not happy!

"Tom, I have one question. What happened?"

"A student accused a teacher of improperly touching him as he made the rounds checking on the children. I didn't believe it at first, but checked it out and confronted the teacher. He fainted when we confronted him, so I don't know any of the details."

"I want to know all the details and why you continued with the program when you knew something inappropriate was happening," the superintendent demanded.

"We isolated the teacher and continued the program because we thought it would be more difficult if we stopped the program in the middle of the week. If I were you, I would get the parents from their cabin and discuss the charges with them."

"You're in no position to tell me what to do! You haven't given me enough information to help me understand this problem. I have to deal with the public. What more do you have to say?"

"I have nothing more to say," I responded.

"Then get out of here! I will deal with you later. The trip should have been canceled!"

Although I had done nothing wrong, I felt the full wrath of our superintendent, who was not happy with me.

There were a few times in my teaching career when I was put on guard by the actions of my superintendent and the principals I had in the building where I taught. I respected their authority even though they made me feel as if I was doing something that was against the law when in fact I wasn't. When I asked for clarification about what specifically I was doing that was wrong in their eyes, they could not provide me with anything tangible and always resorted to letting me know that the district lawyers were looking at things. I guess that is supposed to be intimidating. What "things" they meant, I never knew. I think I frustrated some of the administration regarding the activities I was doing because there were faith-related things involved. When we are teaching, we are told we can't say anything about the Bible, God, Jesus, or Christianity. In reality, within the laws of the land, you can. I also didn't care about my reputation or my job. I focused on trying to walk in a way that pleased Jesus and trusted into His hands all that He provided me with in the form of employment. This is what freed me up to be who I am in Christ and kept me from worrying about what might happen to me. God is in control of all things, even when others think they are.

The day after being confronted by our superintendent, I talked to our teachers' attorney, who advised me to tell our superintendent everything I knew about the situation. I was under his authority and he needed to know every circumstance that happened. I went to the district office and asked to see our superintendent. I apologized to him and told him everything I knew about the situation. After quite a long dialogue, he softened and understood where I was coming from.

God gave you the insight and discernment to know what you ought to do and you humbly followed through on it, resulting in a positive outcome.

Our principal was out of town when all these things happened. He called me into his office and said, "If you hadn't gone to the district center and talked to our superintendent, your job would have been on the line. As it is, he appreciated your position on this difficult matter."

My colleague was called to court and faced a judge concerning these charges. To this day, I don't know exactly what happened. However, he was removed from his position as a teacher and had to serve many hours of community service. I still stay in touch with him and he is my friend.

During a Saturday leader's meeting for BSF the weekend following these unfortunate events, our team became aware of the struggle I was facing at work. One of the leaders suggested that we abandon our agenda and pray for me. The men spent two hours in prayer, interceding for me. Their prayers were powerful and encouraging. Through their prayers and support, I eventually gained the respect of our superintendent, who did not go after me. Even so, there was a time when I thought my career was over.

A second attack the enemy hurled at me was against my family. Our son Mike realized his dream and was selected to attend the Air Force Academy. When I took him to the airport and said goodbye, I felt empty inside. I went for a walk and wondered how I would respond not seeing my son very often for four years. I was excited for him, but for some reason I felt unsure.

When Mike went through the basic training that summer, we weren't allowed to hear from him very often. Toward the end of the summer, he called us and sounded terrible. His voice was weak, and he wanted to come home. I knew something was wrong, so I called and talked to an individual at the Air Force Academy. She explained that our son had hit the wall, as many other students had, and would be all right. We didn't hear from him for several weeks, so we called to inquire how he was doing. We were told he was not at the Academy any longer and was at the psych ward at a hospital in Denver.

I was upset and asked, "When were you going to call us and let us know what was happening to our son?"

"You were on the list and we were planning to call you shortly, but we have a backlog of students struggling, so it takes time to get a hold of every parent."

The next day, Sandy and I boarded a plane for Colorado. We immediately went to the hospital. Mike was in a room with a guard at the door and bars on the windows. I looked inside and saw a thin young man with a short haircut on his knees. He came out to see us and said, "I'll trust you and Mom but nobody else ever again."

We talked to him and he was in tough shape. He said, "Get me out of here! It's like One Flew Over the Cuckoo's Nest." We tried to see the psychiatrist, but he was too busy to talk to us. We made an appointment with him for the next day.

We checked in at a motel and spent the night praying. I lost it emotionally and was really in rough shape. Seeing my son like this was too much for me. I never dreamed anything like this would happen to him. Sandy said, "Tom, you have to pull yourself together Tom, or we'll never get our son home."

The next morning, we met the psychiatrist. He said he was busy and didn't have more than five minutes to talk to us. Then he said, "Your son belongs to the Air Force Academy, and I don't want you messing with my patient."

He said the wrong thing to my wife. I won't quote her word-for-word, but I'll tell you that she undressed him verbally.

"Your patient? We're talking about my son…!"

The psychiatrist called the Air Force Academy and said, "Release this young man or we will have a lawsuit on our hands."

They drove us to the Air Force Academy. After several hours and signing many papers, Mike was released. Now we had to get him home. He refused to get on the plane, but finally we talked him into it. We thought we could take good care of Mike back in his home environment, thinking he would be fine in a few weeks. We were wrong. It took a whole year for him to overcome this tragedy in his life. I won't go through all the details, but we were a family in crisis.

I remember this time and the talks we had about Mike and his behaviors. It was a difficult time. I realized the best thing I could do was continue in prayer for you, Sandy, Katie, and Mike. Crises like these force us to our knees, where we learn to be dependent on God who hears our prayers and answers according to His will. It's never easy, but in the end each crisis builds character that we would not normally possess.

It took hard work and prayer for Mike to recover. I met with an elder at my church and explained the situation Mike was in. He understood because he had a daughter that suffered with depression.

He asked me to meet him the following Wednesday at 8:00 a.m. with my Bible. We sat in his basement for eight hours praying and quoting Scripture back and forth.

"Your son's gonna be all right," he said, after we had prayed all day.

I asked him how he knew.

"I just know!" he said.

Two weeks later Mike asked to see a psychiatrist. They put him on a drug called lithium. A week later, he was his old self again. It was hard to believe. He enrolled at Bethel college and, after a few setbacks, graduated with honors. He also played on the hockey and tennis team. That was a good place for him to recover.

I introduced him to my student teacher at the time, whose name was Becky. I told Mike that I'd seen Becky operate under pressure and that she was a great person. I pressured Mike to ask her out. He replied, "I don't need your help, Dad."

Finally, I gave my son thirty dollars to take Becky on a date. Mike called her and she accepted his invitation. Four months later, they were engaged. A year later, they were married on my birthday. God works in mysterious ways. Mike would've never met Becky had he stayed in the Air Force. She's a wonderful, Christian woman and a perfect choice for Mike. She is the answer to my prayers that God would provide His choice for my son. And He did!

Mike and Becky have been married for 27 years and have three children: a boy and two girls. We are blessed with three wonderful grandchildren through Mike and Becky. Besides that, they bought a house next to ours and we are neighbors. God has a way of thwarting the enemy and answering our prayers above and beyond anything we can expect or imagine.

As I was in BSF, there were many other attacks as well. None of them were easy, but God was with me through them all.

Marriage and Ministry

One October afternoon in 1990, Chris stopped by my school for an unexpected visit. He had a slight smile on his face, which told me he was up to something. It surprised me slightly to see Chris walk through the door of my classroom as I was sitting at my desk relaxing after a rough day teaching.

"Chris, what brings you into my classroom this afternoon?" I questioned.

"How are ya doing?" Chris responded lightheartedly, ignoring my question.

"I'm a little tired after a long day, but other than that I'm okay. What's on your mind?"

"Why do you think I have something on my mind?"

"Because I know you."

"How would you like to take a little trip with me to Luck, Wisconsin?"

"Now, why would you be going to Luck?"

"I'll tell you on the way."

"It sounds like you have something important to tell me. First, I need to check it out with Sandy," I replied.

I talked to Sandy and she gave me the green light. As we hopped in to Chris's car, I was dying to hear what Chris had on his mind that would bring him to Luck, Wisconsin of all places, which was in a small town on Highway 8.

The weekend before I went to see Tom at school, I was up most of the nights planning. I was planning a surprise birthday party for Deb, but as I planned her surprise birthday party, I realized what I actually wanted to do was ask her to marry me. That sent me in a whole new direction. A friend of mine that Deb and I knew through a mission trip to Russia suggested a restaurant to take Deb to on her birthday. It was in Luck, Wisconsin. I brought our friends into the know about what I was planning. They were thrilled to be a part of it. I lined up a limo and rented a tux for the evening.

"All right, what's the big secret?"

"I thought we could have a nice dinner together and check out this restaurant."

"Why this restaurant?"

"Because I'm bringing my girlfriend Debbie and her mother, brother, and sister from California to this restaurant in Luck to ask for her hand in marriage. I had to tell her mom what I was up to, in order to get her on a plane… she's never flown before."

"Are you kidding me?"

"No, I'm serious! I would like you with me when I pop the question."

On the way to the restaurant, Chris told me a funny story. One evening, he realized he really did not want to remain single and that he wanted to have a family. That gave him the courage to decide he wanted to marry Debbie, who he had been dating and fell in love with. He stayed up all night planning how he was going to ask her to marry him. The next day, he called the man who he thought was Debbie's dad. Now Debbie had grown up not knowing her dad. For the first time at the age of 26, Deb had flown from Minneapolis to meet her father. She went hesitantly at the time, but Chris had encouraged her to make that connection and took steps to support her decision. He dropped Deb off at the airport and prayed for her while she was gone. Knowing a little background about Deb and her dad, I listened as Chris told me his humorous experience. Apparently, Chris got on the phone with the man who he thought was Deb's dad. Chris introduced himself and then launched into asking permission to marry Debbie. When he was done, a long pause ensued and then a voice on the other end said, "Well son, that's all fine and dandy with me, but I think you need to call my son. I'm her grandpa." I laughed pretty hard when I heard this part of his story. Chris did call the right man in the end, who gave Chris permission to marry Debbie and eventually walked his daughter down the aisle.

Yeah, that was a bit embarrassing, but I got over it and pressed on with another phone call...this time to the right man.

When we arrived at the restaurant, we talked to the manager and got everyone on board with Chris's plan.

On January 11, 1991, Chris asked Debbie to marry him at that restaurant in Luck, Wisconsin. For some reason, he was running very late as we all waited at the restaurant in anticipation of their arrival.

Haus, the limo driver, picked me up in Richfield right on time. Then we picked up Deb, who was very surprised when I pulled up in the limo to take her out for her birthday dressed to the gills in a tuxedo. She knew we were going to have dinner with our friends Tony and Nancy Nasvik who lived in the Hudson, Wisconsin area. We headed out to pick them up and lost a lot of time when Haus got turned around and lost his way. Once we finally picked up Tony and Nancy, we were way behind schedule and a lot of people were waiting on us at the restaurant.

The restaurant is known for their ribs, but by the time Chris and Debbie arrived, they were all out of ribs.

At the restaurant, we were all huddled around a corner away from the entrance. After Chris and Deb entered, Chris let Deb go in first. As she came around the corner, she was met with a huge surprise to see all of us present: many of the EPPIC team members, some of Chris's family members, and Deb's family from California whom she hadn't seen in a while. When she saw her family members, she was totally surprised and the tears started to flow.

We ordered food and enjoyed a nice meal. Then came dessert: a birthday cake! The staff wheeled the cake out to our tables and stopped in front of Debbie and Chris. Atop the cake was an opened engagement ring box with a sign sitting before it which read, "Happy Birthday...Will you marry me?". Chris got down on his knees and proposed to Debbie. With tears in her eyes, she whispered into Chris's ear, "I don't think so." Then she said, "Of course, I'll marry you! Yes!"

For a moment, that about took my breath away until she finally whispered "of course" into my ear. Relief!

Then, someone from the restaurant hollered out, "Well, did she say "Yes?"

The whole restaurant began cheering and clapping. A reporter for the Eden Prairie News got wind of what Chris did to propose to Debbie and wrote an article about it for a special Valentine's Day edition in the paper.

Chris and Debbie got married on March 29, 1991. At the ceremony, they sang to each other. They sang "I Will be Here" by Steven Curtis Chapman. They sounded pretty good, but Debbie had the stronger voice.

Sometimes I get myself into places I should not be. Singing in front of a crowd is one of them. My voice gave away how scared I was, but Deb's beautiful voice gave me the strength I needed to continue and finish the song with maybe a word or two misplaced within the piece.

I had the privilege of being Chris's best man. The marriage ceremony was held at Wooddale Church in Eden Prairie. Chris was 34 and Debbie was 25 years old.

During the reception, some of Chris's friends did a mime sketch and I entertained the audience with some yo-yo tricks. Sandy and Katie helped by serving in the kitchen. Deb's mom and half-sister helped with the decorations. Chris and Deb drove off in a rented Limo and spent their honeymoon in Cancun, Mexico.

We rented a Volkswagen bug and stayed in two places down the coast along the Gulf of Mexico. It was all very magical and memorable in many different ways. Deb got very sick after we returned home from a bug she picked up in Cancun. Not fun.

While EPPIC had its offices and training areas at the Edina Community Center, Chris and Deb lived in two homes that were both on Wooddale Avenue in Edina.

The first home served its purpose as we got married and eventually brought Christina home. In that home, we housed some of our full-time team members. Once, we even housed six people from Costa Rica as we trained them to form their own mime ministry crew. The second home was an ideal place for us to live and house EPPIC team members as we practiced and performed locally, nationally and internationally. It was much more spacious and had a double car garage and its own driveway. Our first place didn't have a garage and we shared the driveway with our neighbor to the south. We were seriously considering how we might purchase this second property when the basement flooded during a time that the city of Edina surprisingly experienced a deluge of water that flowed into many basements in the area. Reluctantly, we transitioned out of that property and spent about nine months at a house in

South Minneapolis that a couple owned and operated to house missionaries for short periods of time.

When Chris decided to leave teaching, it was a huge change! He was in a career that he loved and had the security of a salary, vacation time, benefits, and hospitalization. He felt God called him to be an evangelist and spread the gospel around the world. He and Debbie were a great team. Chris handled the logistics and traveled extensively with the team, while Debbie did a lot of the training and took care of the kids. She was a gifted performer and a wonderful teacher. They recruited a full-time team who lived with them. Each team member had to raise their own financial support.

We put a great deal of effort into EPPIC's ministry. I traveled around the world with the mime group sharing the gospel using translators in areas that had never heard the message of Jesus Christ. It was a lot of responsibility to live with and train a team while raising a family. Members of the team would help with the children by babysitting and doing various things for our family. We also recruited team members to serve as nannies for our childcare needs, both at home and while we traveled.

In 1997, Chris's family moved to a more permanent location, specifically a hobby farm in Corcoran, which is a northwestern suburb of Minneapolis. The kids loved this environment and its seclusion. It was a great area for them to grow, develop, and learn.

Christina, Jessica and Michaela

Chris has three incredible daughters.

Christina Anne Erickson was born December 4, 1993. Jessica Danielle Erickson was born May 15, 1997, and Michaela Arielle Erickson was born May 29, 2001.

I consistently and faithfully prayed for Chris's children even before they were born. Before Christina was born, Chris kept a journal of each day of his wife's pregnancy. He kept this journal and gave it to Christina on her 15th birthday. I was present at Christina's birth. Chris wanted me there for moral support and prayer.

It was a smooth and easy delivery for Deb. Christina was born prematurely. She was so small that I could hold her whole body with one hand. She was sent to a unit for special care for premature babies. I left Deb's side after the birth to be with Christina while she was being cared for in this unit. A nurse was trying to find a vein to place a needle in her little arm,

but she was so small the nurse was having a hard time finding the vein. After trying nine times, she was ready to find another nurse to give it a try. I looked at her and asked her to try one more time, saying, "I'll pray that you find it this time. You can do it." The nurse looked at me curiously and tried for the tenth time. Relieved, a big smile came across the nurse's face as she successfully found a vein. I dubbed Christina "Pincushion" and often referred to her as "my little pincushion" due to this experience. I also often called her "my little glow worm" because she had jaundice and had to spend time wrapped in a blanket that glowed.

Out of Chris's three daughters, I spent most of my time with Christina since she was the oldest. Chris would bring her to a lot of events where I would interact with her. Chris, Debbie, and Christina spent some time at our cabin when she was a toddler before her siblings were born. She enjoyed that time and loved the water.

I took a few photos of our time at Tom's cabin. Looking at those photos later while preparing to write our story, I noticed that Christina's bathing suit was on backwards. Dads are known for the things they do…and don't do. Naturally, I was the culprit who put her suit on backwards.

Jessica arrived on the scene in May 1997. Chris brought home some tulips he bought in Amsterdam as he returned from an outreach in Croatia. He planted them in a flower bed under the back kitchen window at their home in Edina.

Those tulips bloomed the day we brought Jessi home from the hospital. I nicknamed Jessi "Tulip" to remember this event in her life.

While she was growing up, I spent some time with Jessi at the farm.

Jessi loved the animals, especially the kittens and cats. I referred to Jessi as our cat-whisperer because she was the one who gentled all the barn cats and took care of the kittens when they were born. She had some very special cats over the years. Jessi was also a tomboy, always wearing overalls and hanging out with me in the pole barn. She would always follow me around when I was working outside. Invariably, I would turn around without knowing she was behind me and elbow her in the head accidentally.

I enjoyed interacting with Jessi and watching her grow and develop. Often when I stopped over to see Chris, he would be homeschooling his kids. I did a little tutoring and spent some time helping Jessi with her educational activities. When she got older, she enrolled in Minnetonka High School as a freshman. She did very well academically and athletically. I enjoyed going with Chris to watch her run the hundred-yard dash and pole vault.

I knew Jessi was fast. Speed is what you need as a sprinter and a pole vaulter. One day when Jessi was very young, I was working out in the field and I heard her start yelling at the top of her lungs. As I looked up, Jessi came screaming over this

little hill by the side of the barn with two big roosters chasing her down. She ran straight as an arrow right up into my arms with a terrified look on her face. I've never seen a child run so fast. Before she would run the 100 in high school, I would tell her to "run like the roosters were chasing her." She knew what I meant.

Another May baby came on May 29, 2001.

Michaela was born with a full head of hair and a big voice!

Chris was on an outreach to Kazakhstan and Turkey. It was feared that he may miss the birth of his third child.

That was weighing heavily on me when the crew and I arrived in Turkey. As a result, after discussing the matter with the mime crew, I decided to head home and entrusted the team to continue the ministry planned in Turkey. I set out from Turkey, somehow skirted a strike at an airport in Germany, and miraculously caught a plane to Amsterdam. From there I made a quick connection to Minneapolis. When I arrived at the Minneapolis/St. Paul airport, I didn't have a ride out to my home in Corcoran. As I deplaned and rounded a corner, I ran into a missionary friend named Dave Morton. Dave asked me what I was up to and after hearing me recount the past 24 hours, Dave volunteered to drive me all the way out to the farm. When I arrived unannounced at the door, our nanny Masha and Deb started crying. It was a total surprise that I didn't try to plan. It just happened. The mime crew arrived

two weeks later and Michaela arrived a week after that. So much for saving the day.

Michaela was the only one who earned her nickname.

I called her "Ladybug" because one day she was observed eating one. I think she liked them because they were crunchy. You could not leave Michaela alone with an animal when she was little. A baby rabbit and a baby bird met their demise in her little hands. She just liked to squeeze those fussy and feathery little things, but just a bit too hard. Michaela was the one who would often observe something and then, in a very profound and innocent way, put into words what she was experiencing. There was a time that a friend gave the girls and me tickets to see the Minnesota Twins play. They were great seats behind home plate. We got to the game a little late. As we walked into the row where our seats were at, Michaela looked around. Noticing all the peanut shells on the ground, she exclaimed, "Daddy…there's a mouse in here!" It brought on a round of laughter from all that heard her. Sometimes a child's perspective is so refreshing.

Ministry can take its toll on family life and relationships. Chris and Deb housed multiple team members in their home, often at the same time. Undoubtedly, it was a stressor to always have people around critiquing their marriage, parenting skills, and ministry decisions. Eventually, some things happened that negatively affected Chris and Debbie's relationship. One night, after a big argument, Deb left with the girls and stayed away for twelve days with some family friends. Then, she moved in with another family. Christina was eight years old when Debbie separated from Chris in February 2002. Early on in the separation, Chris and Debbie worked out a plan to take care of the kids and continue their homeschooling as Deb went back to school to obtain a certificate to be a massage therapist. The plan they developed became the girls' routine through their growing up years. During this time, Chris started substitute teaching in the Buffalo School District to bring in more income.

We shared responsibility for homeschooling the girls when they were younger. I remained on the farm in Corcoran, while Deb moved around to various places in the Minneapolis area. I remember coming home after meeting with one of our pastors where a decision was made for Deb to come back to the farm with the girls and for me to move out and find another place to live. As I drove home to the farm, I was very troubled. By the time I got home, I could hardly breathe. I was having a panic attack. This was something I had never ever experienced before. I went into the house, got down on my knees in our living room, and starting praying. I asked the Lord what was going on with me! On my knees before the Lord, I asked Him whether I should move out or not and very clearly heard, "I want you to stay here." In that moment, I realized I had made the wrong decision before Deb and our pastor, thinking it was the right thing to do. As soon as I realized the Lord was directing me to stay put, my spirit calmed down. I remained where I was, quiet and still, for a long time. I called my pastor that night and told him what had happened and that I wasn't supposed to move

out of the house. It was the right thing to do for a variety of reasons. It allowed me to substitute teach within the Buffalo School District. All their schools were three to fifteen minutes away from the property in Corcoran. It gave the girls a stable place to call home as they were growing up: a place that was already their home, and a place that they lived on and enjoyed for almost all of their childhood. Since the property was 13 acres, there was a lot of room for the girls to enjoy, but it also involved a lot of work to maintain the place and to take care of the animals we had. This would have been a challenge for Deb to manage herself, even with the girls to help. I learned later that there were also legal reasons why I needed to stay on the property. It was in fact a place that Deb chose to leave, so it really did not make much sense for me to leave only to have her move out later. I'm thankful that the Lord instructed me to stay as it became a place for the girls and me to heal through the course of the separation and the divorce that was finalized in 2008. We lived on the farm until August 2017, when I remarried and moved after calling it home for 20 years. By that time, Christina had moved out and was starting her photography business, Jessi was newly married, and Michaela was approaching her senior year at Minnetonka High School.

As Christina grew, I would spend time interacting, talking, and praying with her. We had many discussions. After she graduated from Minnetonka High School, we were able to have some great conversations about her spiritual journey. It was very encouraging to see a young woman following the Lord.

Christina was accepted into the University of Missouri at Missoula and then decided to take a gap year and attend Holsby Bible School in Holsbybrunn, Sweden. This is one of the schools that is part of the Torchbearers International organization. Her decision was a complete surprise, but effectively alleviated my concerns connected with the finances related to attending the University of Missouri at Missoula. I was able to pay for the Torchbearer school and all the related expenses by substitute teaching and with the help of an inheritance I received from one of my aunts who passed away.

While Christina was attending Holsbybrunn, we wrote back and forth on many occasions. I told her to guard her heart and not give it away too easily. She met a young man there and I believe they fell in love. They stayed in touch after that year was over. He was from Canada and much of their interaction was through mail and email. He came to Minnesota and we went out to dinner together and had a long discussion. I felt he was a fine young man and a good fit for Christina. However, that relationship didn't work out and she had to overcome a broken heart.

I heard about this young man while he and Christina were at Holsbybrunn. Eventually, I met him when I went to visit Christina in Sweden on my birthday. He seemed like a nice guy, but I wasn't convinced he was the one for Christina. When Christina returned home, she was committed to being in a relationship with him. It became a long-distance relationship, during which I witnessed my true romantic of a daughter go through some very emotional stuff. The guy came and visited

Christina at the farm. They seemed to really enjoy being with each other. Christina and I went to one of her Holsbybrunn friends' weddings in Canada that Christina's boyfriend also attended. During that time, I took him out for dinner, inquired about his intentions towards Christina, and had the "dad talk" with him. He assured me he had nothing but good intentions towards Christina. After that meeting, I still didn't feel right about the relationship, but I didn't tell Christina because she seemed to think it was right. Then she went to visit him during Christmas and stayed with his family. She had a great time, but on the night before she was leaving to return home, the young man informed her that he didn't think they should continue in the relationship. I can't remember all the details Christina shared with me, but I do remember how proud I was of her for the resolve she had and the very mature way she handled the situation. She knew who she was in Christ and I was impressed with the confidence she had in her identity in Christ. The whole experience might have shaken her, but it did not rock her world. Instead, she moved on and grew from the experience. Christina is a deeply grounded spiritual woman who loves Jesus Christ with her whole being. I told her later that I didn't think the guy from Canada was good for her. She practically lectured me on how I needed to be honest with her about guys in her life, because she valued what I thought and honestly wanted my opinion. I learned my lesson and now when asked, I tell her honestly how I feel.

Christina spent a semester at Moody Bible Institute and did very well. College was very expensive and she didn't want to get into debt. So she and her dad decided to discontinue attending Moody, return home, and look for a job instead. She did a lot of nannying and worked in a senior citizens' home before following her heart's desire to start a photography business. She developed Steena Anne Photography and is doing extremely well in this career.

All three of my girls participated in track at Minnetonka High School. Christina and Jessi were captains for the girls' track and field team. They had amazing leadership skills and warm, encouraging personalities. Michaela decided to be a pole vaulter and went out for track her junior year. All three lettered in track and did well in their studies.

Christina and Jessi often traveled with the EPPIC teams Chris and Deb led to various parts of the United States and around the world. They were both excellent mime artists at very young ages. Jessi got involved with EPPIC more extensively and currently serves as a trainer for EPPIC, teaching others mime technique and EPPIC sketch material. She is gifted in this area and does very well acting out the mime sketches. Michaela is also involved in EPPIC. She has great expression and is a main part of EPPIC's local mime crew. All three are excellent performers with great stage presence and intuition as to how to engage in and play their roles. They love helping their dad in his ministry with EPPIC and have all traveled to different countries to present the gospel using mime.

During Jessi's college days, she met a young man from Florida named Austin. Austin came to Minnesota to work in the

clubhouse for the Minnesota Twins. At first Jessi thought Austin was interested in Christina, but Austin soon made it very clear that he was interested in her. He was out at the farm one night and mentioned that he had a desire to be mentored by an older Christian guy. Hearing this, I responded and said, "I can do that." We started meeting and have developed a great relationship with each other. During one of these meetings, I could tell Austin was a little nervous for some reason. At the very end of the meeting, he said he wanted to talk to me. He then proceeded to ask me for my permission to ask Jessi to marry him. We had a little conversation where I strung him along for a bit, but it was an easy decision on my part because Jessi had already told me that Austin was the one for her, and in my heart I knew it to be true. Austin is an incredible Christ-centered young man with an astounding work ethic and a very creative side. Later, we went camping together around Gooseberry Falls where he planned to ask Jessi to marry him. I was able to witness the event personally while Christina photographed the occasion and our friend Josh Flom videotaped it. I was hiding in the bushes above the falls being eaten by mosquitos and witnessed it all!

Jessi introduced me to Austin and I was impressed with his character. I met with him in a restaurant and we had a conversation about his relationship with Jessi. They were quite serious in their relationship with each other at that time. I also talked to Jessi out at the farm about her relationship with Austin. She was truly in love and was considering marriage. I clearly remember talking to both of them about the responsibilities they had towards each other and the challenges of marriage. I was impressed at their maturity level and Christian values.

Jessi and Austin had a beautiful outdoor wedding on Friday, June 2, 2017 in a great setting on a farm in Southern Minnesota.

It was an outstanding Christian wedding and very impressive. I said a few words at the reception and wrote them a heartfelt letter based on my 54 years of marriage, using my experience as a guideline.

They are happily married and live in Mankato, Minnesota. Austin continues working for the Minnesota Twins organization and Jessi is attending the Minnesota State University at Mankato, where she is majoring in Dance and Sports Medicine. Both Austin and Jessi help with EPPIC's ministry.

I haven't been able to spend as much time with Michaela as I did with her older sisters. However, she knows about the friendship I have with her dad. She also knows that I pray for her every day. She has graduated from Minnetonka High School and is an outstanding young lady. She loves the Lord and is very mature in her faith. She's attending Minneapolis Community Technical College and wants be a film director. I hope to spend more time with Michaela in the future.

Michaela is doing great. While she's going to school, she also works as a manager at Sebastian Joe's and volunteers to operate a camera for the services at church. She recently passed her

driver's test and has obtained her driver's license. She's a crew member for EPPIC Minnesota's mime ministry crew. She has a great eye for video and is a very creative individual. I love spending time with her and enjoy her personality.

Chris and Debbie have done an outstanding job raising their three girls who are beautiful both inside and out. They love each other and their parents, despite the divorce. Chris had to step up in his parenting and be more of a father to his girls. He taught them character, responsibility, and life skills as they grew and developed. They each know how to abide with the Lord and have a serious relationship with God. They have a strong spiritual foundation, which will help them be successful as they move into their adult years. I am impressed with all three girls. Chris loves his daughters and they love him! It has been fun for me to see Chris in his role as a father and to have a small part in their developmental process as well.

The Farm and Divorce

Chris and Debbie dedicated their energy to serving God, training a team, and traveling around the world, all while raising their three children. Debbie would either stay home with the children while Chris traveled or she would travel and perform with the team with family in tow. They did this for about nine years after marrying in 1991.

Things began to change in their relationship when they were transitioning from one full-time team to another full-time team. During this time of recruiting and training, both Chris and Debbie went through a very stressful time involving a participant they recruited from overseas. This team member didn't quite understand all that went into getting her to the United States to serve on EPPIC's team and created problems for the organization and the team that was training together. It seemed the enemy of their souls was attacking Chris and Deb.

As a couple involved in ministry, we had experienced the enemy's attacks many times before, but these attacks always involved logistical issues and things outside of our marriage. Deb and I both had issues that we brought into our marriage, family

life, and ministry, but we just didn't have the wherewithal to effectively turn the tables on those issues. Eventually, these problems caught up to us and the enemy used them to divide us and destroy our marriage.

The things that were causing me to stumble were different than what Deb was dealing with, but both of us carried these things into our marriage unknowingly. My baggage had to do with believing a lie about myself that was related to my heart condition. I didn't fully understand the dynamic of my own issues until after Deb had separated.

Later, after a difficult and heated argument, Debbie left the house with the girls and lived with friends for a while. Chris wanted to keep the marriage intact. They went through 15 months of counseling that did not help to restore the marriage and subsequently remained separated for 8 years. The divorce was finalized in 2008.

This was undoubtedly the most difficult time of my life and probably Deb's as well.

Chris and Debbie worked out a routine for the girls, which they established between themselves. The children spent Sunday through Wednesday evening with Deb and Wednesday evening through Sunday afternoon with Chris. They exchanged the children at church. During this time, Chris and Debbie homeschooled the three girls.

I continued to live on the hobby farm in Corcoran with the girls. I wanted them to have a sense of security and a place

to call home. I wanted them to have their own room in that home. We lived in a small solid house on top of a little hill. I jokingly would say that you could get to any room in the house in eight steps from the side entry door. The front of the house faced the wetlands area to the north. There was an old barn and a couple other storage buildings on the property. It was a beautiful setting with farmland, marshes, and homes separated by some distance. It was secluded and private. We would often see wild animals on the property. Deer, fox, pheasants, rabbits, skunks, hawks, eagles, and turkeys were common sightings. It was a quiet, peaceful area to raise the girls. When the girls were home it was a time of creativity, responsibility, and adventure. The girls had space and freedom to grow and develop. When they were home, I was a very busy single dad. When they were away, I was a pretty lonely bachelor. For the first two months when I left them at church for their mom to pick them up, I would literally cry most of the drive home. It was like an adult version of a child's separation anxiety. Eventually though, this became our weekly routine and reality.

Chris was with the girls in most of their extracurricular activities because he had them every weekend when these activities took place.

When they were with me, the girls had responsibility for the animals that we cared for on the farm. When we first came to the farm, we had a cat named Gambier that we brought with us from Minneapolis. There were already other cats on the property when we arrived. Over the years, we have had hundreds of cats, some of which were very special and endearing to each of the girls. More than a few times, we came across litters of kittens neatly tucked away, hidden amongst the hay in some secretive corner of the barn. Then, I added two goats that I purchased from a nearby farm. We named the two goats Skittles and Waddles. They were curious little beasts that got into everything. I built a chicken coop and we raised chicks and started a flock. At one point we were collecting 20 eggs a day. It was fun to search for eggs or watch in anticipation for eggs a hen was sitting on to hatch. Later, we added two golden retrievers which we named Sammy and Caramel. Then, in partnership with a neighbor, we purchased two sheep that eventually grew into a flock of 13. The last lamb born on the farm needed a little help in the birthing process. The girls and I were able to assist. This happened on Easter Sunday just before we went to church, so we named the little lamb Resurrection. My friend and I had the sheep sheared and sold the wool for a little profit. The girls got to watch the whole process. We had a horse named Snickers which I bought for Christina when she was ten years old. Before I purchased the horse, Christina had to do a study on horses and learn about how to care for a horse. She was ecstatic when we finally brought "Snickers Slippers in the Snow" home. Together, we trained Snickers ourselves. You learn a lot about yourself when you spend time training a horse. Christina bought another dog from my good friend John Bergh. She named her Miera. Miera eventually gave birth to 10 puppies! We kept three of them and sold the rest. With all these animals, the girls gained responsibility, learned about the cycle of birth, life and death, and practiced loving and caring for a portion of God's creation.

The farm was a place where the girls grew close to their father. It was one place where their character was formed, their integrity developed, and their spirituality established. This place helped them deal with their parents' separation and divorce which can be so devastating in the lives of children. This was a place of security and steadiness for the girls. Debbie continued to be a great mother to her girls, but I have not been a part of that side of things.

The farm and church were both places that helped the girls as they spent divided time between their mother and me. The girls would be in church every Sunday and Wednesday, which helped build a strong Christian foundation. The church also helped financially with camps and special outings for the girls. They grew up at church and benefited greatly from all the Christ-centered experiences they participated in over the years.

I love both Chris and Debbie and was saddened by their divorce. Next to loving Jesus, marriage should be our highest priority. They both worked very hard in their ministry of sharing the gospel message. That kind of pressure, along with raising three children, did not give them much time to nurture their relationship with each other. They had many great moments in their marriage loving each other and serving the Lord. They raised three godly, beautiful daughters who love both their mom and dad. Even among Christian parents, things don't always work out. Chris and Debbie have both moved on in their lives and spiritual journeys.

Lisa

With Chris's children now growing into adulthood, he focused more on EPPIC Ministries over the next eight years. He also strengthened his abiding in the Lord through his daily quiet times. But Chris was also struggling with remaining single and getting frustrated with a few attempts at beginning a new relationship. After some unsuccessful dating, Chris decided to give this aspect of his life to the Lord.

I got so frustrated with myself and the whole dating scene. I let my feelings start to dictate my actions, and it was a struggle to remain on the right side of the Lord. The Lord took all my mistakes in the dating area and funneled me into a place where he wanted me. After a few months trying to cultivate a relationship with a Christian gal I was interested in, she informed me that God told her I wasn't the one for her. I'm not one to argue with God. After this, I told the Lord I was done with what I was trying to do my way, done with the dating scene, and just wanted to focus on my daughters and ministry.

Shortly after this decision, Chris became acquainted with Lisa. He saw her often at church, a place where he purposed not to be entertaining any romantic relationships.

I suppose it wasn't the right decision, but I didn't want to meet anyone at church. I thought that if I did, I would have to deal with all the awkwardness of being with someone in a place where my children were active and their mother was known. Early on when I started dating, I agreed to meet a gal from church after the final service was over, thinking that the kids would be gone by then. I determined not to talk to my kids about any dating I was doing until a point in time that I knew things were serious enough to share the relationship with them. We agreed to meet in a common area of the church. I was sitting with this gal having a conversation when I felt a tap on my shoulder from someone behind me. I turned around and sat there face-to-face with my youngest daughter Michaela. She said, "Hi Dad, who's this?" Awkwardly, I introduced this gal to Michaela. Then my middle daughter Jessi came up, and then their mom came up. Suddenly, I was right where I didn't want to be with a gal I was meeting for the first time! They all left, leaving me to apologize to this lady for the awkward encounter. Then as we sat and tried to have a conversation, two of my oldest daughter's good friends came and sat by us. I suggested we go sit in another area that wasn't within earshot of Christina's friends. A short time after moving, two more of Christina's friends came and sat on the floor right across from where we were sitting. I leaned over to the gal and, with a smile on my face, asked her if she would like to go to lunch. She agreed and we headed out with Christina's friends looking

on. I took her to a restaurant just down the road from church. As I pulled into the parking lot, there was only one other car in the lot. We walked into the restaurant and sat down at a table near the fireplace. As soon as we sat down, I heard someone say, "Hey Chris!"

There sitting across from me was the chairman of EPPIC's board of directors and his wife. They were the only two other people in the establishment! So much for trying to keep my dating life under wraps. The Lord was teaching me a lesson, but He had to bring me full circle before l came to the realization that He had a plan for me that was better than anything I could put together.

Michaela, Chris's youngest daughter, was acquainted with Trent, Lisa's son.

I observed Trent before I ever met Lisa. He was a loud, crazy, outgoing young guy, often the center of attention. I think Michaela liked that about him. He made her laugh. I first realized Lisa was Trent's mom when she offered me an extra Valentine's Day cookie that Trent had purchased for her. I just happened to be standing nearby when she graciously offered it to me. I hesitantly took it from her, but appreciated her thoughtfulness.

On one occasion, Chris noticed Lisa reading the Wall Street Journal, with her laptop open and papers spread all over the table. He approached her and said, "It looks like you're reading something heavy."

Actually, I said, "What are you doing?"

"I need to read the journal to keep up with things related to my job," Lisa responded.

"Wow! It must be some impressive job."

"Not really. I need to work as a single parent to support my two boys."

It was a short beginning into a new relationship for Chris. In a way, Lisa was an answer to my prayers for Chris. I had been praying for his finances and that he might move from the farm and minimize his expenses.

The very next weekend, the same encounter occurred. This time Lisa was sitting in a different spot, but doing the same thing. Chris approached her, knowing this time what she was doing, and Lisa invited him to sit down. During that conversation, Chris asked Lisa if she was interested in going out for a cup of coffee.

"Yes!" she responded.

No, she said, "I'd like that!"

That cup of coffee turned into dinner and was followed by a long, serious conversation. Chris cut quick to matters that were important to him and listened intently to Lisa's responses and questions. She was a very good conversationalist. He didn't call her back for two weeks, but then called and asked if she wanted to go see a movie together. Lisa agreed hesitantly because it seemed to take Chris a long time to call her after their first date. After just a few short weeks of seeing one another, Chris went on a three-week mission trip to Guatemala and then Honduras. While he was there, they texted one another often.

It was through this back and forth banter that I fell in love with Lisa. I enjoyed her sense of humor, playfulness, quick wit, and her commitment to the Lord and His mission. At one point Mark Warder, the senior high youth pastor, noticed me being in front of the computer and on my phone more than usual and asked me what I was doing. I told him I was communicating with a gal I met and went on a couple of dates with. He said, "You're dating someone?" I admitted I was. He asked me who I was dating, wondering if it was anyone he knew. I asked him if he knew Lisa Kopp. He said, "Lisa Kopp! You're dating Lisa Kopp? Wow, that is so cool!" Mark's positive affirmation helped me feel that the Lord was in this relationship. I told him that I believed I was falling in love with her.

Things moved quickly after that. They became serious in their relationship. They even began talking about marriage. They discussed Chris's three girls and Lisa's two boys.

One evening, Chris invited me to have dinner with him and Lisa at Perkin's Restaurant. When I first met Lisa, I was impressed with her character. She was warm, bright, friendly, and easy to talk to. She treated me warmly.

You've described her very well, Tom.

I felt Chris must have told her about our friendship. During our dinner, I wanted to know her story.

"Are you from Minnesota?" I asked.

"No, I grew up in Indianapolis, Indiana and graduated from high school there."

"Is that where your parents are from?"

"My parents are from China and then they moved to Taiwan when the communists took over. My grandfather had a car dealership in Taiwan and did very well. When my parents were older, they moved to the United States. They met here in the states when they were going to college, married, and then I was born in 1965."

"Do you have any siblings?"

"Yes, I'm the oldest with two younger sisters."

"Did you go to college?"

"Yes, and I have a degree in business."

"Where did you begin your career?"

"My first job was in New York. I didn't like the atmosphere there, so I got a job in Seattle, Washington. It was in Seattle that I got married and had my two boys, Trevor and Trent. My marriage didn't work out, so I took a job in Minnesota with US Bank," Lisa responded.

"Can you tell me about your faith journey?"

"I learned about the gospel of Jesus Christ from friends in high school. It was there that I accepted the Lord as my personal Savior. Now, I have a few questions for you," Lisa said.

"Go ahead, ask away."

"How long have you known Chris?"

"We've been friends for over 40 years. I met Chris on a canoe trip when he was in high school. I was a teacher and he was a student. We began a friendship that has lasted over a long period of time. We are close friends and Christian brothers."

"What can you tell me about him?"

"What do you want to know?"

"Everything!"

"Wow! That's a tall order," I laughed.

"You had your turn. Now don't you think it's my turn?"

"Absolutely! Well, I've never had a better friend. We have a lot in common. We enjoy hanging out together. He loves action and being outdoors and so do I. He accepted Christ in my backyard and now we are Christian brothers. We've been through some tough times together and helped each other out through prayer and dialogue. I trust him with my life and he's always had my back. I could go on and on, but I think you get the picture."

"I sure do, Tom. Thank you for that wonderful answer!"

As we parted company, I had a great feeling about this relationship.

In November, while I was in Florida playing baseball, I called Lisa's dad for permission to ask Lisa to marry me. Her parents expressed some reservations, but her dad eventually gave me permission to ask her. At that point, I wasn't sure when I was going to ask her because my middle daughter, Jessica, was going to get married in June, and Lisa and I didn't want to take anything away from that event in her life by getting married before then.

Later, Chris gave me a great honor by asking me to come to the farm for dinner on his birthday. Lisa and her two boys would be there as well as two of Chris's daughters. It was there he surprised us all and asked Lisa to be his wife.

That was on Saturday, February 4th when we all gathered to celebrate my 60th birthday. It was a surprise to everyone. Looking back, I should have prepared my girls in advance. Although Christina wasn't there at the time, Jessi was stunned and I'm sure Michaela was not happy. I believe they both were expecting me to tell them what I was up to and would have welcomed the opportunity to talk about it and process the information. What they didn't know is that I was growing uneasy about the time between when I asked Lisa's dad's permission to marry her and the time that went by before actually doing that. I did want it to be a surprise to everyone, but underestimated the impact that surprise had on everyone.

It was a great evening to be with Chris's and Lisa's families. Chis and Lisa were married that following August.

The date was Friday, August 11th, 2017 to be exact. Our pastor friend, Mark Warder, married us. All our children were together; my son-in-law Austin was there, Christina's and Michaela's boyfriends attended, and my good friend Phil Peikes came with his wife Sandy, who did the photography. Neither of us wanted to have a big wedding and enjoyed the intimacy and simplicity of just our children and a few friends attending.

I'm truly blessed, Tom. Lisa is a Godsend. Right when I was ready to give up on the idea of marrying again, God put her right in front of me, even though she was there all the time! Sometimes He has to bring you full circle in order to recognize the blessings and benefits He bestows on us when we seek to honor and glorify Him. He took all my mistakes in this particular area of my life and used them all to funnel me into a place where I was open to what He had on His mind for me...and that was Lisa and her two boys, Trevor and Trent. I'm reminded of Proverbs 18:22, which says, "He who finds a wife finds what is good and receives favor from the Lord." I'm thankful that our children have successfully navigated another person in each of their lives. Blending two families together is not an easy matter, but because of the character of our children, it has been a positive transition for us all.

Tom's Retirement

In the year 2000, I retired from teaching. I had 34 wonderful years of ministering to and loving my students. I feel a Christian teacher in the public school has a wonderful opportunity in the classroom to emulate Jesus Christ. I had God's truth in the Bible as my standard and guide as I interacted with my students. I had the indwelt Holy Spirit to guide me. He gave me the power to let each person in my classroom know they were loved individually with love only God can provide.

I chose to be an elementary teacher so that I could have more time interacting with my students for the entire day. I couldn't preach or use the Bible per se, but I could teach its principles and values. I did this every day just by being me. I also worked hard to know each student personally as I worked with them throughout the year. Chris was one student who became a strong believer, a Christian brother, and a close friend. I could tell stories of many other students throughout the years, but this book is about Chris and our friendship.

In my final year of teaching, I had open heart surgery. I had a hole in my heart the size of a nickel. A blood clot went through the hole, causing me to suffer a small stroke. It affected my vision, but only temporarily. My sight came back the next day and the only side effect of the stroke I experience today is numbness in my right hand. I had open heart surgery in January and was out of the classroom for two months. I returned to the classroom in March and finished my final year of teaching.

That still amazes me! I'm the one with the bad valve and need to have open heart surgery someday, not you. Remember when I was 16 and found out about my heart? I told you about it and you must have told your brothers about it, because the next time we were together they took me aside and prayed for my heart valve to be healed. I wasn't a Christian then, and it was admittedly a strange experience for me at that time. I remember the look on your face as they were doing this. You looked very apprehensive, almost apologetic for what they were doing. But I must admit...I haven't had to have open heart surgery yet, so maybe their prayers had an effect.

I never thought of it that way...maybe.

When I returned to my classroom in March, I was reading one of the books I wrote called Brucey Gravy to my students. It is a true story about my relationship with a friend from my childhood to graduation from high school. My students enjoyed listening to the story about my friendship with Bruce. It was about growing up with a friend and enjoying the good times as well as the struggles in a friendship.

It is a great book and I love the title!

As I was reading to my classroom one day, a colleague walked into my room and listened while I read a few pages from the book. After school, she approached me and asked about the book I was reading. I told her that it was a book about my life growing up. She asked for a copy of the book and read it over the weekend.

"Tom, I read your book and couldn't put it down. I would like my students to have a project of writing your story into a script with dialogue and make it into a play," she said.

"Jean, I don't know what to say! I'm glad you enjoyed the book, but writing it into a play would be a huge challenge, wouldn't it?"

"Tom, I work with gifted students. I try to think outside the box and come up with a challenging experience for them. My students would love to write a script from your book and it would be a great project and learning experience! We would write dialogue and make it into a play and a perform it for our student body."

"I don't know what to say!"

"Just say yes!" Jean responded.

"Yes!"

"Tom, this is your last year teaching. I want my students to learn and highlight your career as well. It would be our way of thanking you for the gift you gave this community for your efforts and dedication as a wonderful, gifted teacher."

"I don't know what to say. I'm speechless! If you think you can pull it off, go for it!"

What happened next involved the entire school and community. They had auditions, selected parts for individuals from students in the third, fourth, and fifth grades. They taught them not only lines to memorize, but songs to sing. Classroom teachers, the music teacher, and specialists all got involved. Parents also helped with costumes and background scenes. Teachers allowed students to leave their classroom to practice their parts.

As Jean was working on this project, she approached me in the hall. "Tom, who are you? Everyone I ask is thrilled to be a part of this performance."

I was asked to be the narrator of this play. When the director thought the play was ready, we performed it for the student body. We received a standing ovation from the audience!

We sent a letter to the community informing them that we were giving an evening performance based on an original book by Mr. Thomas Hall. There was such a response that we had to perform three nights in a row in our gymnasium, which had a stage to work on.

On one of the nights before the play, I was sitting at a table signing books for people. A lady came up and handed me a book and asked me to autograph it and write it to "Joseph, Haley, and Olivia." I laughed and told her,

"No way! Those are the names of my grandkids."

"Dad!" she said. I looked up and was shocked to see my daughter, Katie, standing in front of me. She had flown in from Maryland for the event. I was thrilled!

The last evening was so packed that some people had to watch it from closed circuit screens in the classrooms. That evening, I invited my entire family, friends, and my fifth-grade teacher, Mr. Capetz. In one scene which was about my experience in fifth grade, the director stopped the performance and said, "Mr. Hall's fifth grade teacher is here tonight. Mr. Capetz, would you please stand up and face the audience." He got a loud thundering applause. I watched as tears streamed down his face. It was quite moving for all of us to see.

A cable company from our community filmed this last performance. This event was on closed circuit television for over a month. Chris also got involved. He had already left teaching and was sharing the gospel through mime performances all over the world at the time. He helped with the lighting, sound, and even makeup with some of the students in the play.

During the play, the music teacher and director asked Bruce and Terry, two of my childhood friends, to come to the front. They came up and each of the teachers took hold of each of them and started dancing during the play. I didn't think they had it in them, but they both did a great job.

At the end of the play, the director asked my family to come forward. I introduced each of them. They were all part of my story as well.

After the final performance was over, we gathered in the media center. Unbeknownst to me, my colleagues arranged for a cake and drinks for a retirement party. My colleague, Ron, narrated this event and after some funny stories, he invited anyone who wanted to speak to come to the front. Many people came up to speak. It was kind of embarrassing, but also encouraging. The speech I will never forget came from my daughter, Katie. Before she spoke she whispered to me, "Daddy, why didn't you tell me about this? I would've prepared something." She got to the microphone with all the poise in the world and a huge smile on her face. She opened with the line that set the tone, "I have the greatest daddy in the world…"

My son, Michael, also spoke but got emotional and had a hard time finishing his speech. Chris also said some kind words about our enduring friendship.

It was a fun experience and everyone at the school was totally involved. I enjoyed having a small hand in the production and, like Mike, I probably got a little emotional as well.

The next day, several colleagues came up to me and were impressed with my daughter's speech. They wanted to know how I raised a daughter that loved me so much.

I ended the retirement party with a few words of gratitude. As I was speaking, I saw my entire class sitting in the back of the IMC listening to everything. It was an evening I will never forget and a great way to end my career.

Where We're At Today

On the last day of school, I cleared out my desk. All the lesson plans and things I needed were not important anymore. My life was about to change drastically. I threw everything away. As I walked through the building for the last time, I got emotional. I had been told I could never teach. I'm grateful for the college counselor who went to bat for me and allowed me to enter the college of education with mediocre grades. I received my teaching degree and had three wonderful years teaching in the state of California and 31 years teaching in the Mounds View School District. I proved the critics wrong! I had a wonderful, satisfying, and rewarding career. I gave it my best shot. God wanted me to be a teacher and helped me have a wonderful career with students who made it all very rewarding. Sandy was also a huge part of my success. I give all the glory to my Savior and Redeemer. I was 59 years old when I retired.

I did my best as a classroom teacher. When I turned my career over to God and asked for His help every day, I became more effective as a Christian teacher. He helped me give my students a great education. I took my job seriously and understood the responsibility I had towards teaching each of my students. I taught my students with passion and put my whole heart into it every day. I followed the curriculum, taught values, gave illustrations, told stories, and tried to relate everything to life. I emphasized character and reputation. I tried to teach each student to have a strong work ethic and give their best effort to each assignment that I gave them. I gave them this quote: "Your work is a self-portrait, so sign it with excellence!"

I like that phrase!

I worked hard at trying to get to know each of my students personally. I met each of them at the door with a handshake in the morning. I talked to each one of them individually and asked them questions about their life during our morning break. I talked to a different student each day and kept notes as to what we talked about.

After my 34 years were over, I tried to evaluate my career. I loved teaching! My strength was relating to my students, which I consider to be a gift from God, not something developed out of my own education. I will never fully know the impact I have had on the students I've taught over the years, but I know that with God's help, I was able to change lives for the better and help my students develop skills they could build on as they moved through the educational system.

Retirement has been an interesting time for me. I no longer have to work to put food on the table and pay the bills. The pressure is off and I no longer need to perform. The first couple of years of my retirement, I did some long-term subbing and private tutoring. I wondered how my life with Sandy would change. I realized Sandy and I would be alone together all day long. I didn't know where to start. I took the time to explain to Chris how I was adjusting to this time in my life. We've always been there for each other and this never changed in our relationship even as I retired.

My response was… "Dude, enjoy it!" Secretly, I did have thoughts about how Sandy was going to put up with having you around so much.

Sandy and I had some adjustments to make. It helped that each of us had our individual spaces in our home. Sandy has the whole upstairs and I have the basement. I spend a great deal of time down in the basement where I have my desk and computer.

Sandy has great organizational skills. She handles all our finances and keeps our home in order. We also own a cabin in Wisconsin with my brothers. Sandy pays all the bills and keeps everything going in that endeavor as well. We made our three-season porch into a year-round family room. We have two reclining chairs and a small couch in that room. It is carpeted with a small electric fireplace. It's a place we both love to go to read and relax. We both have a personal quiet time with the Lord that we really enjoy.

I spend a lot of my time in the basement at my desk. It's where I spend my time with the Lord. I read the Bible and pray every day. I've read the Bible from cover to cover many times. This year I'm listening to the Bible on audio as I follow along in my One Year Bible. As I listen to this presentation, I often stop the dictation and write my thoughts in the margin of the Bible. God is opening up his Word to me in a new way with this method. I also spend time with a book written by Oswald Chambers entitled, My Utmost for His Highest. I read a short devotional from the Daily Light Devotional by Anne Graham Lotz, which is all Scripture. My children and grandchildren are reading Daily Light as well, so each of us are in this same portion of Scripture together every day.

This one-on-one time with the Lord has been incredible. I spend most of each morning in the word of God and in prayer. Sometimes I work out physically as well, though I'm not as consistent exercising as I am practicing my spiritual exercises. I like flexing those muscles more.

Me too! Lisa is into exercising each morning and has been a great influence on me to do the same. I try to do some weights, cardio, and swim at least every other day. But my devotional time remains more important.

In my retirement, my ministry has drastically changed. I attend two Bible studies. One is with 12 to 15 guys who meet at Perkins Restaurant every other week. We are studying different books in the Bible. Chris comes to this study with me. These men were part of my youth. They all received Christ later in life and are hungry for God's Word. I love this group of guys because each of them are real, open, and honest with their struggles in life.

I also attend Bible Study Fellowship, the study I was in charge of for many years. We have 500 men and 60 children in our group, which meets every Monday night. We meet from September to June each year. This year I'm carpooling with my friend Kerm, his son-in-law Tom, and another friend, Andy.

I met Andy when I was a teacher. He accompanied me on a week-long field trip to an environmental camp. Andy and I became friends. He was a Christian at the time, but was not growing in his faith journey. I invited him to Bible Study Fellowship for about ten years before he agreed to go. Andy has been in Bible Study Fellowship for about four years now. He is a very successful businessman. He owned a waste management company. He sold his company and now is involved in buying hotels and office buildings. I disciple Andy in the summer to help us both stay in God's Word.

The ministry I'm most involved with in my retirement is discipleship. I've discipled three men recently over the phone. I'm taking them through the Design for Discipleship program Chris and I went through. I am currently working with a man that I met on a golf outing. He lives in Cedar Rapids, Iowa, so I disciple him remotely. We meet every other week during the school year. He's a successful businessman with a family and two grown children. This year we are in the fourth book of the DFD series. We will finish the program this year. My goal is to get him into God's word and help him grow spiritually. I also worked with a young man who lives in Washington State. We spent three years together on the phone studying God's Word and praying together. He is currently a lieutenant in the United States Air Force. It is encouraging to know that I can still relate with young Christian men.

I also discipled my son-in-law Jason for a short time over the phone. He is a doctor and colonel in the Army. One evening, as we were finishing our discipleship time, he asked me how he could pray for me. I thought about it before giving him my answer.

"Jason, Sandy and I have been married for many years. Although we each have devotions individually, we've never had devotions together. She's resisted my attempts and said we have our own private devotions and that's enough." I said.

"I'll be praying for you every day!"

"It's probably too late for us, Jason."

"It's never too late!" was his reply.

The following week, I approached Sandy.

"Let's have devotions together," I suggested.

"Tom, we don't have to do devotions together. You have your quiet time and I have mine. It's personal for us and we don't need to have it together."

"Yes, we do, Sandy. I really want to do this with you!"

"Who have you been talking to?" Sandy questioned.

"Jason is praying for us!"

"So, you want his prayer to be answered." Then with a smile on her face she said, "So that's why you're pushing so hard."

"No, that's not the only reason… but it would be nice if his prayers were answered!"

"All right! We will begin tomorrow morning."

We began by reading a devotional called Our Daily Bread. We're also reading a book that's entitled The Many Names of God by Tony Evans. We've been doing daily devotions for close to two years now. I read from two devotionals and we pray together. We use the acronym ACTS (Adoration, Confession, Thanksgiving, Supplication) to direct our prayers. We use this method to pray for each other as well as for our children and grandchildren. When Sandy hears me pray for her and thank God for her as his precious gift to me, she knows how much I love and appreciate her. She's heard things that I've said to God about my feelings toward her that I've never shared with her before. It's really impacting our marriage in a positive way.

This time together has been amazing! God has heard us worship and thank him together, He's also heard our confessions. He has answered many of our prayers. I'm sorry that we started this discipline so late in our marriage, but Jason was right…it's never too late!

Because of your testimony about having some devotional time with Sandy, Lisa and I have started reading a book together called New Morning Mercies. Christina, my oldest daughter gave us each a copy and it's a very well-written and insightful devotional book. Both of us have benefited by reading it. After reading it, Lisa and I talk about it. It is ministering to both of us and gives us the opportunity each day to connect with each other and discuss what the Lord is doing in our lives. Our

schedules are very different, so we have to work at making this a priority and finding the time to share with each other our responses to the reading with each other.

Between my two children, Sandy and I enjoy the company of 15 grandchildren.

I tell people this all the time when they talk about their grandchildren. I say, "My good friend Tom has two kids. His son Mike has three kids and his daughter, Katie, has 12. Between the two of them they have 15 kids! That's 15 grandkids!"

These children have become my main focus. Sandy and I spend much time with Katie's family during the winter months. I'm currently discipling Katie and her four adult children through Design for Discipleship. We are currently in book 6. We'll finish the series this winter. My challenge to each of them is to disciple others in the same series. There's no homework because they have each gone through the series and have answered all the questions. They just need to buy a blank book and pray for another person interested in growing spiritually that they can disciple. Just think, if each of them discipled one person each year and challenged that person to disciple another, the multiplication effect would be tremendous! Thousands would not only receive salvation, but help others grow and develop in their faith journey as well.

God has given me the opportunity to disciple my grandkids in a few different ways. A couple years ago,

Mike's 15-year-old daughter Amy gave me a call on the phone.

"Grandpa, this is your granddaughter, Amy."

"Hi Amy! What's up?"

"I would like you to disciple me and teach me how to do homiletics."

I jumped all over that one.

"Absolutely, Amy!"

We met for over the summer. I thought her homiletics were excellent. We studied the book of Galatians together.

As we went through God's Word together, I was amazed at her maturity and passion for the Lord.

Her older sister, Rachel, called me on the phone and wanted to know about baptism. I called my brother Bob, who is a pastor in New York. He sent me some excellent material on baptism. I spent many hours talking to Rachel about baptism. She took notes on everything I said. She is a student and loves to learn.

During the summer, we invited her other grandparents and relatives to come to our cabin. We all gathered together in a circle on the front lawn. I gave a short talk on baptism. Joseph, one of Katie's sons, led us in a beautiful prayer. We sang some songs and prayed together. Her father and I took Rachel out into the lake to baptize her in the name of the Father, Son, and Holy Spirit. She had put all her notes from our Bible study about baptism into a spiral notebook. I read her comments about baptism. I have never met anyone more prepared for baptism than Rachel. It was a thrill for Mike and me to baptize Rachel in our lake, a place she loves. We are not pastors, but we are followers of Jesus Christ, and I believe we are qualified to baptize younger believers.

I came to the same conclusion when a mime crew member asked me to baptize him when we were doing evangelistic work on the beaches in Florida. He is the only person I've ever baptized.

Ryan and Amy, Rachel's siblings, were baptized in a local church. Rachel is quiet and deep. This baptism for her and our family was unique and personal.

I have never been bored in my retirement. I've written and published five books. I'm currently working on two more books. This book is one of them!

As I am writing about my spiritual journey in my retirement, Chris is also very active in ministry, discipling other younger men and serving his family and church.

I've continued serving the Lord through EPPIC Ministries International and now manage six different mime ministry teams in different parts of the world. It's my desire to use "The Gospel in Mime" tool more extensively and strategically in outreach work worldwide. I'm currently recruiting individuals to serve on a full-time mime ministry crew working through EPPIC to engage in evangelistic outreach ministry and to help establish more mime crews in other places in the world. Time will tell if this all comes to fruition. I'm in my second marriage, currently enjoying a relationship with a wonderful gal named Lisa whose two sons have joined my three daughters to form a blended family of seven. Parenting is always a challenge, but at the same time a complete joy.

We are proud of our children and take great pleasure in each and every one of them. I find myself surrounded by young men these days, both within the family and outside of the family. With almost all of them I'm enjoying a discipleship relationship wherein we all are growing in our relationship with Jesus Christ and with each other. I presently have the privilege of knowing and spending time with a great group of guys: our boys Trevor and Trent, my son-in-law Austin, my daughters' past and present boyfriends, different guys from past and present mime crews, and a young man I met through a local ministry. There are others I'm praying for...others I desire to see come to faith in Jesus Christ. Again, time will tell. I'm dabbling in writing both for personal and ministry reasons. I'm no longer officiating high school varsity soccer or substitute teaching in the public school, and last year was probably my final year playing hockey. I do, however, continue to play baseball in my spare time and enjoy the camaraderie of men from all walks of life. Shout-out to the Minnetonka Mustangs in the 35 and over Federal League and the Loretto Mets in the 50 and over league. Keep donating baseball equipment to the baseball ministry in Guatemala, but more importantly, consider your relationship with God and find a more intimate one with Him through His Son Jesus Christ by placing your faith and your trust in Him and all that He has done for you and for me.

Chris and I are always close to each other. We're just a phone call away. We still get together often and our conversation is usually very deep. His girls are all grown now and very godly women. Chris is close to all his children. He and his wife Lisa have a great marriage, and she is helping him in ministry even as she works full time.

The process of writing this book has brought Chris and I even closer together. We spent much time and energy discussing all the topics of our lives in this book. We have laughed over stories told and things remembered. I hope you see how our relationship began, grew, and developed. God used each of our gifts and talents to serve him. We still love to get together, have coffee, hang out, and interact with each other. God has greatly blessed me by allowing me to have a friend like Chris. I'm grateful! He brought us together 47 years ago and I believe we will be serving God together into eternity. Amen!

Ditto!

Reflections

Little did I know when I met Chris what the future would hold for us. Now that I'm in my old age and Chris is in his sixties, we have a pretty incredible story to share. It's a story of two men wanting direction and meaning in their lives.

When we met, I was a nominal Christian with very little purpose in my life. Chris was an unbeliever and not interested in any kind of religion. The outdoors brought us together. We both loved the wilderness that was untouched by human hands. Was this a divine appointment or a chance meeting? God's word says in Ephesians 2:10, "For we are God's handiwork, created in Christ Jesus to do good works, which God prepared in advance for us to do." I'm convinced that by God's sovereignty, Chris and I were brought together.

After six years of friendship, God performed an impossible miracle in my back yard. I happened to be the messenger, but God the Holy Spirit was the director. Chris recognized the sin in his life and needed guidance and direction. I shared the gospel with Chris and he became a believer. God put this good work in front of me to do. He spoke through me and saved Chris.

From that moment on, our friendship deepened, and together we both grew spiritually. We shared and enjoyed the same faith. We developed a love for one another that gave freely and expected nothing in return. We truly understood each other. We shared generously with each other. We had new goals together. The focus was not on ourselves, but on others. We prayed together. We were accountable to each other. We confessed hidden sins and worked together to overcome them. There was nothing hidden between us, no hidden agenda. We were quick to forgive each other when a disagreement arose. No matter what hit us when life got tough, we weathered the storm together.

Everyone has a philosophy by which they live their lives. My personal philosophy for 21 years was "try anything once and if it feels good, do it." This was an experiential lifestyle, and with it came momentary pleasure and lasting guilt. I couldn't find the satisfaction and contentment I desired. If someone were to look at me from the outside, my life would have appeared good. Yet I knew within me things were bad. No one was more aware of my personal wrongdoing than me. As hard as I tried, I couldn't solve my problems on my own.

To my surprise, as my life and circumstances got worse, an attitude developed within me in which I wanted to know God. The problem I faced was not knowing where to begin. God was preparing me to trust Him. He was breaking my pride and self-confidence. I began searching for Him even before Tom ever gave me the Bible. Through Tom's help and the words of the Bible, I came to understand that the guilt I carried was

caused by my own sin. I learned that our holy and pure God has revealed Himself to the world through the person of Jesus Christ. I realized that if I accepted the truth about who Jesus is and what He did for me, God would forgive me of my sin and help me with my problems. After I decided to place my faith in the life and work of Jesus Christ and I confessed my sins to Him, it took only a moment for God to remove the guilt that had piled up within me.

I placed my trust in Jesus Christ at 2:15 a.m. on May 26th, 1979, outside, on my knees, under a big old tree, the stars overhead. I remember this specifically because I had been searching and my search ended here. I wanted to know how to begin a relationship with God and He showed me through my friend Tom. But it took 21 years, a Bible, and a Christian friend to help me find Jesus who has now become my "philosophy of life."

Revelation 3:20 was the first verse in the Bible I ever read. Tom directed me to it. When I read it, I knew God was talking to me, asking whether or not I was going to ask Him into my life. I said "yes" in that moment. Naturally, I sought Tom out concerning all of this and he shared with me the simple yet powerful truth of Jesus Christ, His life, death and resurrection...how He did it all for me to deliver me from my sins. I knew it was right and I wanted to ask for and receive Jesus.

Since that initial experience with Tom, God has been gracious and merciful towards me. Life hasn't become easier, but because of Jesus Christ and the Holy Spirit and His word at work in me, life has purpose and meaning. I'm changing and the changes are good. He has helped me grow in knowledge about Himself and directed me in many ways. God is now a reality to me. Just like spending time with Tom towards developing

our relationship, I spend time with the Lord to develop my relationship with Him. It's a relationship that continues to grow. Now, I can live in a way that pleases God because I'm sure of what He says about Himself. It's a joyful experience to live this way.

God used Chris in my life as much as He used me in Chris's life. God called us both to different ministries where we were stretched and challenged. We needed each other for strength, accountability, and prayer support.

Chris's statement in my backyard came true. "I want to be more spiritually mature than you are at your age!" I was thirty-seven years old at the time. With God's power and the Holy Spirit's work, that statement came true. Chris also told me he wanted to be like an oak tree with thousands of acorns. Thousands have given their lives to Christ as his team has spread the gospel around the world.

I hope reading this book has inspired you to reach out to those in your life who need to hear the gospel message of Jesus Christ, to disciple young believers, and to faithfully serve in whatever capacity God brings to you. Chris and I are truly brothers in Christ. It is our hope that you know Jesus and have experienced His forgiveness, His grace, His love, and His help in your life. Just as God worked in Daniel's life in the Old Testament and Paul's life in the New Testament, He can work in your life as He has worked in ours. Open your heart to Him and He will not disappoint you. Draw near to Him and He will draw near to you.

Conclusion

Every book has an ending. God's Word is no different. The book of Revelation, the last of the 66 books in the Bible, describes God's ending to all things as we know them in this world and the beginning of a new chapter called eternity. The enemy of our souls wants us to believe that the book of Revelation is too hard for anyone to understand. This is a lie. He is also the one who wants you to believe that life can be found outside of the Creator. The Scripture says in Psalm 14:1 that only a fool believes there is no God. God is alive and well. Revelation puts into chronological order God's end game: His plan that He has had in His mind and in His heart from the very beginning to redeem His creation through His grace. God wants to redeem all who believe and by faith receive His promises which are all ours in and through Jesus Christ.

Tom and I both had to answer this question: "Is your name written in the Lamb's Book of Life?" Thankfully, we can both answer this question affirmatively. We know what we know and we are sure of it.

You can be sure your name is written in the Book of Life if you personally confess and repent of your sin and believe in what Jesus Christ has done for you. It is by grace alone, through faith alone, by Christ alone that we are saved. It has nothing to do with being good enough, or doing enough, or having enough faith. Salvation is a free gift that God extends to all who trust in the finished work of His Son, Jesus Christ.

One day, in a hospital room, my dad and I had a conversation as he was going through some serious health issues.

I asked him, "Dad, when you die and find yourself before God and He asks you, 'Why should I let you into heaven?' what would you say?"

"Why, I would tell him that I'm a good man and that I believe in Jesus."

"Dad, from what I understand about it all, the first part of your answer has nothing to do with it and the second part of your answer will bring you all the way home," I told him.

"Really?" he responded.

"Really!" I said.

There are not many roads that lead to God as many people want to believe. There is only one road. Jesus made that very clear when He said in John 14:6, "I am the way and the truth and the life. No one comes to the Father except through me."

If you desire to draw near to God, He will draw near to you according to James 4:8. If you desire to know the one and only true and living God, He can be known through His Son, Jesus Christ. If you desire to know Jesus, he is revealed to you through the Holy Spirit who indwells within you when you place your faith in Jesus. It is the Holy Spirit who will help you understand God's word, the Bible. The Holy Spirit will also help you grow in your relationship with Him.

When my girls were growing up, I had a phrase I used with them to get them to turn a light off when they turned one on, to clean up when they messed up, or put something away after they took something out. That phrase was simple. All I said was, "A to Z, Christina. A to Z. Jessi, not A to M… A to Z. Michaela, finish what you started…A to Z."

God is like this. He is the Alpha and the Omega, the first and the last, the beginning and the end. His plan for you and me began in creation and ends in Revelation. We are to live eternally with Him in His magnificent presence in a new heaven and a new earth, so much better than the one we've experienced. It is the knowledge of God that gives one hope and joy and peace and purpose in this life. All one needs to do is give heed to the one and only Lord God Almighty of the Bible and serve Him only. Run from the stubbornness of heart that keeps one ignorant of the way of God and diligently pursue the knowledge of God. He has a new eternal suit for you that's wrapped in His righteousness and a new name that only He knows. I used to think that my name, Christopher Allan Erickson, was the name He'll look for in the Book of Life. But something inside me is telling me that it is the new name that He has given me, a name I do not yet know, that He will find in the Book of Life. Then the intimacy which I have enjoyed with Him here in this world will be fully enjoyed in His gift of eternity, the beginning of a new life.

Read Isaiah 43:1-13. I dare you.

The story that Tom and I share and have written about here is only one example of what God does in our midst. Tom has in his own words "retired," but I think it is safe to say that one does not retire from walking with the Lord and serving Him. This life is a training ground for eternity, an eternity in which we will worship and serve Jesus Christ, the perfect

Lamb of God, Lord of lords and King of kings. As He said in Revelation 22:13, "I am the Alpha and the Omega, the First and the Last, the Beginning and the End."

Afterword: An Unexpected Ending

I'm writing this with great sadness in my heart. After we finished writing our book together early in 2020, Chris had open heart surgery. After four months of health struggles and multiple surgeries, Chris passed away on July 20, 2020. He will never see the completion of the project we worked on so hard together.

Christina, Chris's oldest daughter, called me to let me know my dearest friend had passed while I was at our lake home in Wisconsin. As I hung up the phone, my heart was filled with sadness. I needed privacy, so I went into our bedroom and began sobbing. My dear friend had lost the courageous battle he fought to stay alive. I know Chis is with his beloved Savior, but I was not prepared for this separation. I am down here on earth and feel suddenly alone.

We had plans to publish this book and use it as a platform to share the gospel around the world. The book is a story of brotherly love and Christian transformation in our lives together. Now that he is gone to be with his precious

Lord and Savior, our dream will never come true in the way I thought. I believe God is bigger, and He can use this book in ways Chris and I never dreamed of.

I left my cabin vacation a day early because I was speaking at Chris's funeral on Friday morning. I had prepared a speech. I thought Chris would not want me to talk about him and instead share the gospel with the audience. However, when I woke up Friday morning, I did not feel peace about my message. Right around this time, my dear friend Mike Buzzell called me to condole me after hearing about Chris's death. He comforted me with kind words and said he wanted to write a prayer for me and email it to me. When I read his email, I was totally convinced to change the speech I was going to make at the funeral. Mike's prayer said everything I needed to say about Chris and his ministry. I decided to focus on our story and then end my speech by reading Mike's prayer.

The funeral was held at Wooddale Church, where Chris had been a member for many years. The audience was limited to about two hundred people and had to be socially distanced because of the coronavirus pandemic. Pastor Richard of Wooddale Church opened up the funeral with a few words,

"Welcome to the celebration of life service for Christopher Allen Erickson. My name is Richard Payne and I am the worldwide missions pastor here at Wooddale Church. I had the privilege of knowing Chris prior to becoming the mission pastor. Your presence today is a blessing to Chris's family and they are so grateful that you are here to support them during these difficult times. I was just shown an image before I walked on where little red dots represent people watching all over the states and the world, so thank you for being online as well as here in person.

"We've gathered here today for several reasons: to honor and celebrate the life and memory of Chris, to grieve his death, and to acknowledge the loss of someone we knew and loved. We've gathered here to give tangible support to his wife Lisa and their blended family: Chris's daughters Christina, Jessica, and Michaela along with Lisa's sons, Trevor and Trent. Also present are other family members, including one of Chris's siblings. And we've also gathered to receive comfort and healing from the one who can provide that. Jesus said in Matthew 11:28, 'Come to me, all you who are weary and burdened, and I will give you rest.' What Jesus said sometimes feels impossible. 'Come to me, all you who are weary and burdened, and I will give you rest.' Soak that in today, I ask, and let Jesus give you rest and comfort."

After saying a beautiful prayer for this time of celebration and reflection, the pastor invited Chris's younger two daughters up to share. Chris's youngest Michaela started.

"We just want say thank you to everyone for taking time to celebrate our Dad Chris's life with us. I'm sure that you're all here either online or socially distanced in the pews because Christopher Allan Erickson had an impact on your life. I've always said he was the kind of man who left an effect on everyone he met, and there is no doubt that he had the light of Jesus shining through him for all the world to see. My sister Jessi and I wanted to take a few minutes to share what made this punk of a kid into the amazing, goofy, God-fearing, kindhearted man that he remains."

After giving a short bio about Chris's childhood and adult life, Michaela continued.

"There were two very crucial people in Chris's life: a man named Tom Hall and Jesus Christ. Tom took Chris under his wing and cared for him like a father. He became Chris's spiritual mentor and had prayed for him, his future, and his walk in faith since the day that they had met. It's because of Tom Hall that our dad became a born-again believer at the age of 22 and it is because of Jesus Christ that he is in eternal glory and happiness as we gather today. He's up there in heaven hooting and hollering just like he did when he burst out of the water on the day that he was baptized. Chris lived his life for God and was one of the most dedicated evangelists I've ever known.

"One of the biggest blessings in his life, he'd always like to remind us of, was becoming a father and having three daughters. He always said he'd be a rich, poor man all of his life because of us. Having three girls isn't easy, but he could've done it one-handed. And let's be real; as a single dad for most of our lives, he often did.

"Around three years ago, he settled into a loving marriage with Lisa and gained two bonus sons, Trent and Trevor. He was so excited to become a father of boys and a husband again, and he loved getting to know his second family and merging our lives together as one. He was so grateful to be able to expand our family and care for Lisa and the boys with open arms.

"God is good and gave our dad a full, fruitful life. If he was here right now, he'd go on and on about God's goodness and how God has a plan for each and every one of us. And you'd better believe that he'd exceed the talking time limit. And I think we might have picked that up from him. He definitely didn't have stage fright. He'd tell us how our plan isn't complete until we're called home. If you woke up today, God's got a purpose for you, and we know Chris's plan was complete. He's done all that God has called him to do and he's home."

Chris's second daughter, Jessi, proceeded to share with everyone present and online what her father went through before passing.

"At 63, he was still playing baseball and hockey, still a full time missionary, still traveling, and still reminding me that he could jump in and perform with the mime team at any moment. In April, a little after Easter, my dad contracted a bacterial blood infection that attacked his heart, and it was clear he needed to have open heart surgery right away. He had his first surgery on Mother's Day. On May 15, he decided to go in again for a second open heart surgery because of the complications that developed. He told each of us that he loved us, and that he was so proud of the godly women we had become. He said that he wasn't afraid and that God had him and that His plan was perfect. We didn't know it, but that was the last time we would hear our daddy's voice. This was followed by a third open heart surgery on May 17. Complications continued and it was decided that in the midst of the riots, he should be transferred to the University of Minnesota

Hospital. The next day, he had a heart attack and had to be rushed into the ER for his fourth open heart surgery in the span of two weeks. I don't know anyone in the world who could've done that! He continued to surprise and baffle the nurses and doctors when he was awake. He was still his feisty old self, trying to pull the breathing tube out so he could talk to us. We always had to remind him that even the toughest of warriors needs support. At every one of these scary milestones, I had a calming and peaceful voice in my head saying it would be okay and to be calm and patient. The voice was reassuring that Dad would be okay but that something bigger was coming. Something that would rattle our hearts, so we buckled down and prepared to weather whatever storm was coming our way.

"We prayed boldly for miracles upon miracles. We kept asking God for one more, just one more, and we saw our prayers being answered. On June 28, the repair on Dad's heart pulled away and my dad's heart started to bleed. He went into a cardiac arrest, and after 30 minutes of CPR, he was rushed into his fifth open heart surgery. The doctors suspected that his brain was without oxygen for ten minutes, suffering extensive brain damage. Due to this, they told us he would pass within the week. My father had to prove them wrong one last time and lived almost three weeks after that statement.

"He passed naturally and peacefully on July 20, surrounded by loved ones. God picks his toughest soldiers for his hardest battles and God couldn't have picked a better man. We are sorry and so extremely sad that our Dad couldn't be here, standing in front of you, telling this incredible story to you himself. But we are so honored and so proud to be able to tell it in his place. Through these past few months, we have seen miracles and the perfect timing of God. He protected our hearts when we needed it and made us strong and resilient when we couldn't have stood alone. We feel the peace only God can give and we have seen our dad show God's grace and faithfulness to others around him without even speaking a word."

After Jessie finished, Chris's oldest daughter walked up to the podium and began to share with the audience.

"My name is Christina Erickson and I am Chris's oldest daughter. To see all of you here and to know that so many of you are seeing this online and hearing our testimonies is a feeling I knew I wouldn't be able to express properly, so thank you for being here.

"When you are forced to reflect on a loved one's life because of death, your eyes are opened to all the aspects of their life, the very edges of their existence, and everyone it encompasses. I am left speechless at the edges of my dad's life and all of the places, people, and stories those edges hold. Thinking about all of you and your histories with him makes me think that his life had an effect that I can't even fully realize yet. His suffering and how unexpectedly short our time with him was is being used even now and has such a glorious and unfathomable purpose, directly impacting our lives and changing them, even after the grave.

"When my dad committed his life to Jesus, a tenacity and driving force came up alongside of him. Looking backwards, it's clear God called my dad just as He calls each of us into a relationship with Him. My dad never turned back in his faith. He always climbed upwards and forwards toward a deeper understanding of Christ and Scripture. He faced trials and challenges that shaped his life and character as we all do, but he never left his relationship with Christ. His pursuit of Christ is the reason so many of you felt drawn by him, loved by him, and affected by him. There is no other reason. It was God who was reaching you, equipping you, and encouraging you using the physical hands and presence of my dad. I guarantee you that no one has felt more reached, more equipped, and more encouraged by my dad than his children.

"As his daughter, my dad was one of the most important people in my life. He was always so verbal and communicative with me. He would call me when he missed me, write me letters whenever I went away from him, and call me beautiful or even better when I made him proud. He would leave notes of encouragement around my room in high school. One I still have says, 'You impress me,' and it's written across an entire sheet of printing paper. Whenever he had a free day or found himself downtown, he would text me to see if he could swing by and get me coffee. I would pause whatever deadline I was working on to go sit with him and update him on my life. He always pursued time with me. He would drop most things to help me. He fixed an uncontrollable car horn at three a.m., found missing hard drives at airports, searched a football field for my wallet, picked me up, dropped me off, and prayed with me. If he could, and I was in need, he gave to me. He helped me practically toward my dreams, but he also spoke of and involved me with his. In my adult years, this was a shift in our conversations that I noted and I held very dearly. I'll miss all of this so much! How easily he gave his words, his time, and the energy I experience with him when we were both absorbing one another's visions. I know beyond a doubt that he loved me-- that he loved all of us-- and he saw me. His love and relationship was incredibly special to me and I mourn the absence it creates in my life. However, in moments of mourning, when the absence finally feels real and it triggers anxiety and loneliness and a deep-rooted grief, I try to remind myself that we are not without hope in our tears.

"We as Christians know and have seen that God does immeasurably more than we can imagine in our lives. We are promised that He works for our benefit even in circumstances of suffering, even when victory doesn't look like your loved one coming home. It's strange, but we naturally display strength in our moments of grief and brokenness because we know that each unforeseen circumstance is orchestrated by a God who loves us and will give more of Himself when we are weak or emptied. With that knowledge, we carry on in difficulties, at times overflowing with joy when it doesn't make sense. We hold all things with open hands with a fierce testimony in our hearts that we follow a God who is trustworthy even when He takes. I will miss my dad so much, but I know he isn't sitting with me in my grief. The beautiful things here on earth: recognition, marriages, babies, financial stability, brilliant relationships with those we love, time… all of those things are not our greatest reward. Our greatest reward, ironically, is found in death and in eventually leaving all those beautiful things behind. As Christians, we will one day be face-to-face with something more sweet and beautiful than anything we experience here on earth… and when we see that glory so closely, we climb upwards and forward with tenacity and a driving force to reach that which is promised to us more quickly. We gladly leave. I'm sure that on this past Monday, my dad gladly left. Remaining here with you all today without him is now just a new opportunity. I now have the opportunity to tell everyone the depth of my dad's faith in Christ, his impact on my life and on others, the love that Jesus has for him as well as for you, and the hope we carry as believers in Christ. That continued opportunity is worth all of this. I'm quite positive that my dad would agree. Thank you."

Chris's wife Lisa gave a beautiful talk by saying,

"Please let me start on behalf of the entire Erickson family with my heartfelt thanks for the prayers, cards, meals, and other incredible help you have provided over the past three months. I also want to call out the skill of Chris's amazing medical team. We are more grateful for these gifts than you can ever know. Many have remarked of our family's resilience and joy. We give credit to the Lord and to the wonderful folks He has put in our lives.

"Your care for us reminds me of Chris's rock-solid character. The thing I loved most about Chris was how he was an example of a life transformed by Christ.

"You may have already read in the program or on the funeral website some of Chris's siblings' fun stories of his childhood. Chris retained a love for adventure and an independent spirit into adulthood. But he allowed Christ to build his rule-following side, so that he could ultimately marry a "by-the-book" person like me. I'll never forget our first two dates, where Chris let that serious side come out. He made sure I knew key things about his background, including the defective heart valve that ultimately lead to his passing. I confess I hung on through the serious talks partially because I thought he looked like Clint Eastwood. I also thought it funny when he told me, "Actually, Clint Eastwood looks like me." Finally, at the end of the second date, he agreed to my request to do something totally fun. We went to a movie for the third date and were off to the races.

"Chris allowed Jesus to shape his heart to disciple many young men over the years. That softening allowed him to be a strong emotional support to me and the children as well. While an avid athlete and person on the social circuit through college, Chris let the Lord hone listening and encouragement skills as he grew. One of my favorite pieces of advice from Chris was him telling me, this overachiever, not to strive when trying to grow, but just to yield when prompted by the Lord's spirit.

"Chris never feared death. Chris had full confidence in a better life through acceptance of Jesus Christ as his Savior. I remember being granted a special privilege to visit Chris before the second of his five open heart surgeries and ten ultimate trips to the operating room. We missed each other, but he was not afraid of the outcome, whether a great life here or in Heaven. That was the last time I saw Chris conscious. But it is a great memory of faith and peace.

"Now that we are past Monday, July 20, 2020, I have peace and joy too among the grieving. I am blessed with our two sons, three daughters, and yes, even the dog, whom I have to admit is pretty cute despite the amount of shedding hair. I had almost three years of a wonderful marriage with a man who made me laugh and relax, who prayed during my every media appearance and big project, and after whom William Dafoe also could claim he got Chris's good looks. God is good. All the time."

One of the most amazing parts of the funeral was when they played a video of Chris talking to his daughter, Christina. In the video, Chris told her that he was going to have open heart surgery in the coming year. It was wonderful to see Chris and hear his voice. Christina was concerned about the danger of open heart surgery. After explaining in the video what he needed done to his heart, Chris said,

"I've learned a lesson. Here's the thing. My valve is tightening and my heart is getting harder. So here's the lesson: that calcification around my valve is like sin in our life. And the more we let sin creep in, the harder our hearts get. And once we come to Christ, He gives us a new heart: a heart of flesh, not a heart of stone. By God's grace, we have all our lives to put our faith in Him and to walk with Him. Whatever our lives entail from beginning to end… could be 62 years, could be 12 years, could be 102 years… but whatever it is, determined by God and His plan for our life, He gives us all that time just to recognize who

He is and receive Him for who He is. The sooner we do that, the better life is. The later we do that, we still enter into eternity with Him, but we don't experience all the joy and the things that come with knowing Him now. So I'm thankful that at the age of 22, I came to Christ, and I've been serving Him and knowing Him all these years. I've sinned and transgressed, but He forgives, and by His grace He keeps bringing me along and allowing me to walk with Him. So, I plan to do that and I have perfect peace going into the surgery. If I die on the table, I know where I'm going. If my life is extended another 20 to 30 years, I know what I'm doing."

Pastor Richard gave a great and moving talk using Chris's words from the video. He prayed the sinner's prayer and asked if anyone listening online or in the audience wanted to become a follower of Jesus Christ to repeat his words. "Lord Jesus, please forgive me of my sins. I believe You died on the cross, was buried, and rose again. I ask You to come into my life to be my Lord and Savior. I want to serve You the rest of my life!"

Lastly, this is what I shared at Chris's funeral. Thankfully, I wasn't overly emotional and I was able to get through it.

"I'm Tom Hall. Chris was more than a friend. I remember riding in the car with him on his birthday and one by one, his three beautiful daughters sent him a message. Since I was in the car, I was able to listen to them. How those girls love their dad is amazing.

"I first met Chris when he was 16 years old." I went on to describe how we met at the Boundary Waters, the same story that this book records. I briefly painted a picture of how our friendship began and how we grew close quickly. I described our relationship throughout his college years and the way he came to Christ in my backyard. Continuing to fight back the tears, I said,

"I have a really close friend who called me at my cabin when Chris died and comforted me. He told me he wanted to write a prayer for me before I talked today. These are his words, but I believe every word of this prayer. See if this doesn't describe Chris. I wish I had written this.

> *Heavenly Father, our hearts are heavy as we come together in spirit to remember our great friend and brother in Christ, Chris Erickson. Chris was a son, a husband, a father, a mentor, a leader, a proclaimer of the good news of hope found in a changing relationship with Jesus Christ. Chris's life displayed before us was filled with the love and passion he found when he made the life-changing decision to welcome the Lord Jesus into his heart. That decision transformed him into a disciple who, by the power of the Spirit, and through the ministry of EPPIC International, was able to share the good news of the gospel literally to the ends of the earth. Chris left a legacy and a life that is well-lived evidenced by the fruit of the Spirit that he modeled for us: love, joy, peace, patience, kindness, goodness, faithfulness, gentleness, and self-control.*

Chris helped us laugh. Chris challenged us to think and reflect on Your kingdom purposes for our lives. He spoke intently, with wisdom, and rarely became angry. In these final months, Chris was encouraged and reminded that the difficulty of these days is fleeting. These light momentary trials achieved for Chris an eternal glory that far outweighs us all. So Chris fixed his eyes not on what is seen, but what is unseen. Chris knew what is seen is temporary, but what is unseen is eternal. His joy is complete. May the memories that Chris has left us grant us joy, celebrating his life, humility, and honor to the Lord. 2 Timothy 4:7-8 reminds us that Chris fought the good fight. He finished the race, he kept the faith, and now there is in store for him the crown of righteousness which is the Lord, the righteous judge, rewarding not only Chris but all who wait for his appearing. The complete joy that Chris has attained is available to all who will come to a saving relationship with the Lord Jesus Christ. May the memory of his life be useful in helping others find the Lord Jesus. To Him who is able to keep us from falling and to present us before His glorious presence without fault and with great joy, to the only God our Savior, be glory, majesty, power and authority on this day and forevermore. To the praise of God's glory, Amen.

Goodbye, my friend. I'm rounding third and headed for home, and I'll see you real soon.

Appendix: Chris's Last Letter to Tom

March 26, 2020

Tom,

My dearest, most beloved brother in Christ, cherished and faithful friend, mentor and spiritual father...this letter has long been brewing in my heart and now overflowing with words far too inadequate for expressing my deepest feelings concerning our relationship with one another these past 47 years.

Amazingly, though we are in different places than when we first met, the same chemistry is present that has marked our friendship from the very beginning. It's definitely a God thing! He ordained our friendship through His mercy and grace, knowing He would use you to "reel me in" at a time when He turned my heart onto Himself and measured out to me the faith in which I now stand. Notwithstanding, mine is a faith cultivated by your persistent prayer for my salvation over a period of six years(!) followed by another three years wherein the Lord used you to help me become a true disciple of Jesus Christ…a believer intent on following the Lord, obeying His word and correctly handling the word of God in order to effectively apply it to my life and ministry.

Your steadfast confidence in me encouraged me to pursue righteousness. Your compassion and sacrificial love extended to me have constantly witnessed God's love to me. You've led me by example and demonstrated to me what it means to be merciful and non-judgmental towards others. You exhibited patience and forbearance with me when I ran ahead of the Lord and thought I knew more than I really did. You've been steadfast in your support of me in ministry, not only financially, but more importantly through prayer and the consistent message, spoken or not, that said, "I believe in you." This simple yet powerful message has carried me, by the grace of God, through my last high school years, four years of college, difficulties in ministry and marriage, as a single dad, and now in the context of a new blended family.

Habits have a way of fixing one's character and character has a way of fixing one's destiny. You helped me build into my life a daily habit of spending time with God. To daily spend time before the Lord in prayer, studying, memorizing, and meditating on His word is a spiritual discipline that reflects the legacy you leave in your grandkids' lives, in the lives of those you've discipled, and in my personal life. My destiny, and yours, is wrapped up in the promise that eternity is ours in and through our belief and faith in Jesus Christ.

As I write this, I know you are in pain in regard to the treatment of cancer spots on your head, face, and neck. I pray that the Lord Jesus will bring healing and health to your body. As you have faithfully prayed for me and my family, know that I am praying for you, Sandy, Mike & Becky, Jason & Katie, all the grandkids: Rachel, Ryan, Amy – Joseph, Haley, Olivia, Grace, Victoria (Tori), Jesse, Jeremiah, Joshua, Trinity, Abigail, Jubilee and Jedidiah (I'll call them "The 12 Disciples"), for your brothers, for Matt, and for the ministry you continue to have in your "retirement."

I want to thank you for taking the time to write our book. May the Lord Jesus Christ continue to bless you and direct you and keep you. May His loving arms strengthen you and uphold you my friend. May His joy be your strength as you let His perfect peace comfort you…that peace that passes all understanding…not as the world gives, but as only He can give. His countenance shines on you, and through you, and it has been and continues to be a light that leads me to the refreshing water of righteousness where you have taught me to drink in and be thankful for His abundant mercy and grace, unto His praise and glory. I love you brother!!

By grace alone,
Through faith alone,
In Christ alone!

Chris

About the Authors

Tom Hall is a retired teacher from the Mounds View School District in New Brighton, Minnesota. He has a great love and respect for children and spent thirty-four years teaching and caring for 5th and 6th grade children. Tom has also directed a Christian camp, and served as a teaching leader in Bible Study Fellowship. He has been married for nearly sixty years and has two children and fifteen grandchildren.

Chris Erickson worked as a teacher for fifteen years before taking a leadership position with EPPIC Ministries. For twenty-five years, Chris served in full-time ministry with EPPIC and traveled all over the world, sharing and proclaiming the Good News of Jesus Christ. Chris passed away on July 20, 2020, and is survived by his beloved wife Lisa, his three daughters, his two stepsons, and beloved friends and family.

Made in the USA
Monee, IL
25 June 2021